The Biblical Seminar
80

The Synoptic Problem

The Synoptic Problem
A Way Through the Maze

Mark Goodacre

SHEFFIELD ACADEMIC PRESS
A Continuum imprint
LONDON • NEW YORK

Copyright © 2001 Sheffield Academic Press
A Continuum imprint

Published by Sheffield Academic Press Ltd
The Tower Building, 11 York Road, London SE1 7NX
71 Lexington Avenue, New York NY 10017-653

www.SheffieldAcademicPress.com
www.continuum-books.com

British Library Cataloguing-in-Publication Data

A catalogue record for this book is available from the British Library

Typeset by Sheffield Academic Press
Printed on acid-free paper in Great Britain by The Cromwell Press, Trowbridge,
Wiltshire

ISBN 1-84127-238-8

CONTENTS

LIST OF FIGURES AND TABLES

For many New Testament scholars, studying the Synoptic Problem is something to avoid at all costs. It is thought to be both complex and irrelevant. Those who do study it are warned not to allow themselves to be dragged into a quagmire from which they may never emerge, and into which they might drag their unwitting students. But those who have devoted time to studying it find the image of a quagmire unsatisfactory, and a more appropriate one that of a maze. Mazes are indeed sometimes complex, but they present a challenge that encourages the excited adventurer to have some fun. And ultimately they promise, after some extensive exploration, that there is a way through. I think that I have found a way through this special maze, and I would like to take you with me.

Though I hope to provide students with a fresh way into a topic that is often thought to be impenetrable, this book is written for anyone with an interest in entering, exploring and emerging from this maze. I have attempted to make it as accessible as possible by translating all the Greek and by being liberal with the use of examples, synopses and summaries, and providing a glossary at the end. This book also has an associated web site (at http://www.ntgateway.com/maze), which provides extra work materials like coloured synopses, links to articles and other materials discussed in the book, and the chance to discuss this book and the issues raised.

The problem will be taken step by step. We begin by looking at what the Synoptic Problem is and why it is worth studying it (Chapter 1), laying out the data as clearly as possible (Chapter 2). The case for the Priority of Mark's Gospel will then be made (Chapter 3) and its ramifications explored (Chapter 4). The intriguing, popular 'Q' hypothesis will be introduced (Chapter 5) and the case against Q presented at the end (Chapter 6).

Readers should be warned that the solution to the Synoptic Problem favoured here (the Farrer Theory) is partly orthodox and partly unorthodox. It argues strongly that Mark's Gospel was the first to be written, but it also argues against the existence of the Q source. This unorthodox stance directly affects only the last third of the book (Chapters 5 and 6), but my hope is that everyone will read the whole book. There are plenty of introductions to the Synoptic Problem that take the standard view for granted, often failing to give an adequate airing to alternative viewpoints. Now, whether or not you are sympathetic to the Q-sceptical view contained here, at least the case against Q is laid out in a sympathetic and straightforward manner.

Finding a way through the maze has been enjoyable for me not least because of my partners on the journey. Long before I began work on this book, my thinking on the Synoptic Problem was strongly influenced by three figures, without any of whom it could not have been written, Ed Sanders, Michael Goulder and John Muddiman. When I was an undergraduate in Oxford, Ed Sanders's lectures on the Synoptic Gospels were fascinating, and I blame him for generating an enthusiasm in me for studying the Synoptics that gets ever stronger. He introduced us to the Synopsis of the Gospels and encouraged us to do lots of colouring, probably the ideal way to immerse oneself in the study of the Synoptics. (I'll be encouraging my readers to do this themselves in due course.) But I am also influenced, far more strongly than he is likely to realize, by my doctoral supervisor John Muddiman of the University of Oxford. And since I began working at the Department of Theology in the University of Birmingham in 1995 I have been lucky enough to spend time talking to and learning from Michael Goulder, who had retired from the Department of Continuing Studies the previous year. My first book, *Goulder and the Gospels*, was all about his ideas. Although I continue to disagree with Michael over several elements in the discussion of the Synoptic Problem, our agreement is much more fundamental. On more than one occasion I have discovered that some great new idea I have had is actually one of Michael's ideas that I'd read once and since forgotten.

The encouragement and intellectual stimulation I have received from others, John Ashton, Stephen Carlson, David Parker, Jeff Peterson, Chris Rowland and Barbara Shellard has also been invaluable.

There are those too with whom I enjoy different yet complimentary journeys, my family and friends, and especially my wife Viola who has helped me to develop many of the insights that are key to my thinking, while at the same time providing me with a route to sanity and a means by which I can be sure to keep my feet on the ground. And the fact that our daughters Emily and Lauren always provide the most enjoyable distraction from my academic work leaves me with no other choice but to dedicate this book to them.

ABBREVIATIONS

ABD	David Noel Freedman (ed.), *The Anchor Bible Dictionary* (New York: Doubleday, 1992)
DBI	*Dictionary of Biblical Interpretation*
ETL	*Ephemerides theologicae lovanienses*
JBL	*Journal of Biblical Literature*
JSNTSup	*Journal for the Study of the New Testament*, Supplement Series
NTS	*New Testament Studies*
SNTSMS	Society for New Testament Studies Monograph Series

Chapter 1

ENTERING THE MAZE:
STUDYING THE SYNOPTIC PROBLEM

1. *Harmonies and Synopses*

The traditional Nativity Play is a familiar part of Christmas—little girls dressed as angels with tinsel halos, shepherds with head-dresses made from tea-towels, kings with glittering crowns made of foil, the Virgin Mary dressed in blue holding a doll, and Joseph, in his dressing gown, looking on. What all such plays have in common is that they are *harmonies* of the biblical accounts of the birth of Jesus. They take some details from Matthew and others from Luke. It is Matthew who stresses the role of Joseph and Luke who concentrates on Mary. It is Matthew who has the magi, Luke the shepherds and angels. Only Matthew has the star in the east; only Luke has the census and the manger. In the Nativity Plays, and for that matter on Christmas cards and advent calendars too, the distinction between Matthew's Gospel and Luke's is an irrelevance. There is one story of the birth of Jesus, and that story is produced by harmonizing the details of each account together.

This is the popular way to read the Gospels. The interest is in the story of Jesus and not in the peculiarities of each of our four canonical Gospels. Most of the Jesus films adopt the same course—they harmonize the events recorded in the Gospels in the attempt to produce a coherent, dramatic narrative. *King of Kings* (1961), *The Greatest Story Ever Told* (1965), *Jesus Christ Superstar* (1973), *Jesus of Nazareth* (1977) and *The Miracle Maker* (2000) all, alike, carefully combine events and details from different Gospels in the service of their narrative. To take just one example, *Jesus Christ Superstar* features a scene in which Mary Magdalene, who is characterized as a prostitute, anoints Jesus not long before his death, and Judas complains about the cost. This draws together several elements from all four Gospels, an anonymous woman anointing Jesus in Mark 14 and Matthew 27; an anonymous 'sinner' woman anointing Jesus in Luke 7; a mention of 'Mary, called Magdalene' just afterwards in Lk. 8.2; Mary of Bethany anointing Jesus in John 12; and Judas complaining about the cost in the same chapter. In watching the simple scene, one would hardly have guessed the extent to which the sources for its several strands are scattered in our canonical Gospels.

This way of reading the Gospels is not simply a recent and popular development. It is the way in which they have been read for most of their history. It proceeds in part from an embarrassment that there should be four Gospels in the Bible and not one. If we are to think of 'gospel truth' and the reliability of Scripture, there might seem to be a problem in the fact that the first four books in the New Testament announce themselves as the Gospels *According to* Matthew, Mark, Luke and John.

This was a problem that was keenly felt from the earliest times and the Church Fathers, from the second century onwards, often engaged in the attempt to 'apologize' for the difficulty. One such character was the apologist Tatian, who dealt with the difficulty at the end of the second century by composing a harmony of all four Gospels entitled the *Diatessaron*, in which details from all four Gospels were woven together with painstaking care. This was the first of many down the centuries. Indeed the heyday of such harmonies was probably the nineteenth century, when bookshelves were awash with books that were, essentially, harmonies of the Gospel accounts presented as *The Life of Jesus*. Even Charles Dickens wrote a pious *Life of our Lord*.

But since the late eighteenth century, the harmonies have had a very important rival. For in 1776, a German scholar, Johann Jakob Griesbach, produced the first *Synopsis* of the Gospels.[1] A *Synopsis* is a book in which parallel accounts in the Gospels are placed side by side for the sake of comparison, like this:

Matthew 8.2	*Mark 1.40*	*Luke 5.12*
And behold, a leper	And a leper	…And behold, a man full of leprosy; and having seen Jesus,
having approached Jesus worshipped him, saying,	came to him, beseeching him and bending his knee, saying,	he fell before his face, saying,

---

1. J.J. Griesbach, *Synopsis Evangeliorum Matthaei, Marci et Lucae* (Halle, 1776).

'Lord, if you will, you are able to cleanse me'.	to him, 'If you will, you are able to cleanse me'.	'Lord, if you will, you are able to cleanse me'.

Now, far from harmonizing the discrepancies, the *Synopsis* actually draws attention to them. One can see at a glance here what is similar in Matthew, Mark and Luke and what is different. Whereas Matthew and Mark talk about 'a leper', Luke refers to 'a man full of leprosy'; whereas in Mark the leper 'beseeches' Jesus, 'bending his knee', in Matthew he 'worshipped him', and so on.

Summary

- The popular tendency when reading the Gospels is to *harmonize* them.
- The Gospels have been read in this way since the second century.
- The Gospels can be read in *Synopsis*, that is, in such a way that different accounts can be compared and contrasted.

2. *The Synoptics and John*

Viewing the Gospels in *Synopsis* has had two key consequences. The first is the birth of the term 'Synoptic Gospels'. The first three Gospels, Matthew, Mark and Luke can be arranged in columns so that they might be 'viewed together' (*syn* = with; *opsis* = look at). The account of the healing of the Leper, quoted above, is not in John. Indeed John features few of the incidents shared by the other three Gospels, and when he does feature a parallel story, such as the Feeding of the Five Thousand (Jn 6), the wording varies so greatly that setting up columns is a very complex matter.

Summary

- Viewing material in Synopsis involves Matthew, Mark and Luke but not John. Matthew, Mark and Luke are therefore called '*Synoptic Gospels*'.

3. *The Literary Relationship of the Synoptics*

The second, related consequence of the appearance of the *Synopsis* is the birth of *the Synoptic Problem* and it is no coincidence that J.J. Griesbach, the scholar who produced the first *Synopsis*, was also the first to provide a critical solution to the Synoptic Problem.[2] Before considering the solutions, however, let us look at the problem. The Synoptic Problem might be defined as *the study of the similarities and differences of the Synoptic Gospels in an attempt to explain their literary relationship.*

It is a fundamental assumption of the study of the Synoptic Problem that the first three Gospels share some kind of literary relationship. In other words, there is some degree of dependence in some direction at a literary level. Occasionally a dissenting voice will sound, but, on the whole, this is a firm consensus in scholarship, and perhaps the last one in the subject—for after this, as we shall see, opinions begin to diverge. This consensus is based on the fact that there is substantial agreement between Matthew, Mark and Luke on matters of language and order. One sees the agreement in language in the example of the leper (above). Often the agreement is close, as in our next example.[3]

Matthew 9.9	Mark 2.14	Luke 5.27
And having passed on from there, Jesus saw a man seated in the tax-office, named Matthew, and he says to him, 'Follow me'. And having arisen, he followed him.	And having passed on he saw Levi son of Alphaeus seated in the tax-office, and he says to him, 'Follow me'. And having arisen, he followed him.	And he saw a tax-collector named Levi seated in the tax-office, and he said to him, 'Follow me'. And having left everything and having arisen, he followed him.

2.   *Commentatio qua Marci Evangelium totum e Matthaei et Lucae commentariis decerptum esse monstratur* (A demonstration that Mark was written after Matthew and Luke) (Jena, 1789–90), in Bernard Orchard and Thomas R.W. Longstaff (eds.), *J.J. Griesbach: Synoptic and Text-Critical Studies 1776-1976* (Cambridge: Cambridge University Press, 1978), pp. 103-35.

3.   The term 'says' in both Matthew and Mark here is known as 'the historic present', a device whereby the evangelists (especially Mark) write about past events in the present tense. I have preferred to keep the translation in the present tense in order that one can see differences between use of tense in the synoptics.

Some have argued that the closeness in agreement between the Synoptics could be due to faithful recording of the committed-to-memory words of Jesus, but significantly, in cases like this, close agreement is not limited to the words of Jesus, and it will not do to argue on this basis that the Gospels are linked only orally. There is agreement in both narrative material and in sayings material.

It is, nevertheless, worth noting just how close some of the agreement in records of speech is among the Gospels—and records not just of Jesus' words. This example comes from the preaching of John the Baptist, this time found only in Matthew and Luke, and so in two columns:

Mt. 3.7-10	*Lk. 3.7-9*
'Offspring of vipers! Who warned you to flee from the coming wrath? Bear fruit therefore worthy of repentance and do not *presume* to say in yourselves, "We have Abraham as father"; for I say to you that God is able from these stones to raise up children to Abraham. Already the axe is laid at the root of the trees; for every tree not producing good fruit is cut down and cast into the fire'.	'Offspring of vipers! Who warned you to flee from the coming wrath? Bear fruit therefore worthy of repentance and do not *begin* to say in yourselves, "We have Abraham as father"; for I say to you that God is able from these stones to raise up children to Abraham. Already the axe is laid at the root of the trees; for every tree not producing good fruit is cut down and cast into the fire'.

The wording is virtually identical—only the word for 'presume' (Matthew) and 'begin' (Luke) differs. Nor is this an isolated instance. The reader who picks up the Synopsis will quickly find at random plenty of examples of close agreement between two or three of the synoptic parallel accounts of given instances.

The thesis that this agreement is due to some kind of literary dependence seems to be quickly confirmed by the matter of order. It is striking that Matthew, Mark and Luke all have substantial similarities in the way in which they structure their gospels. It is not just that they share the broad framework of events, John the Baptist—Baptism—Temptation—Ministry in Galilee—journey to Jerusalem—crucifixion—resurrection. What is noticeable is the extent to which incidents and sayings follow in parallel across two, or sometimes all three Synoptics. Sometimes, these include events that are not in an obvious chronological, cause-and-effect relationship. The following sequence illustrates the point.[4]

Matthew	Mark	Luke	Event
16.13-20	8.27-30	9.18-21	Peter's Confession
16.21-23	8.31-33	9.22	Prediction of the Passion
16.24-28	8.34–9.1	9.23-27	On Discipleship
17.1-8	9.2-8	9.28-36	Transfiguration
17.9-13	9.9-13		Coming of Elijah
17.14-20	9.14-29	9.37-43a	Healing of an Epileptic
17.22-23	9.30-32	9.43b-45	Second Passion Prediction
17.24-27			Temple Tax
18.1-5	9.33-37	9.46-48	Dispute about Greatness
	9.38-41	9.49-50	Strange Exorcist
18.6-9	9.42-48		On Offences

This example, covering just over a chapter in Matthew and Mark, and a little less than a chapter in Luke, is typical. In incident after incident, two or three of the Synoptics agree on order. There is variation, of course. Luke's account of the Rejection at Nazareth is earlier in his Gospel (4.16-30) than the parallel account in Mark (6.1-6a) or Matthew (13.53-8). Matthew's version of the Healing of the Paralytic comes later on (9.1-8) than does that incident in Mark (2.1-12) or Luke (5.17-26). But the order of accounts, or *pericopae*, always converges again after a while. It is usually held that this state of affairs is simply too great either for coincidence or for an orally remembered record. The explanation has to be, on some level, a literary one.

Some, no doubt, will feel that a firmly fixed oral tradition behind the Gospels could explain these data, claiming perhaps that the obsession with written texts is a modern preoccupation. Here, though, we need to notice that there are hints in all three Synoptic Gospels themselves that the connections between them are of a direct, literary kind. First, both Matthew and Mark agree with each other on the interesting narrator's aside in the apocalyptic discourse, 'Let the reader understand' (Mt. 24.15//Mk 13.14, the same three words in Greek). This points clearly and self-consciously to texts that are read[5] and to some kind literary relationship between these two Gospels.

---

4.   Where a space is left, this means that the incident is not in parallel here in the Gospel concerned.

5.   I do not think, however, that we should rule out the possibility, even

Further, Luke's Gospel begins with a literary preface in which he mentions the 'narratives' of his predecessors, implying he sees his task 'to write' a Gospel as being influenced by and critical of their attempts (Lk. 1.1-4). If there is one thing that seems clear, it is that there is some kind of literary relationship among the Synoptic Gospels.

Summary

- Viewing material in Synopsis has given birth to the *Synoptic Problem.*
- The Synoptic Problem is the study of the similarities and differences of the Synoptic Gospels in an attempt to explain their literary relationship.
- The Synoptics feature some very close agreement in both wording and order.
- The scholarly consensus is that this suggests a literary relationship between them.

---

4. *The History of the Investigation*

This literary relationship is what constitutes the Synoptic Problem. As soon as one has noticed the similarities and the differences among the Synoptics, one is naturally eager to find an explanation. Why the varieties in agreement in language and order among them? Could any of the evangelists have known the work of one (or more) of the others? Are they dependent on older, now lost written sources? It is the attempt to answer these questions that has been meat and drink to Synoptic scholars for the last two hundred years or so. Indeed, it could be said that the history of the investigation of the Synoptic Problem is the history of proposed solutions to it.

J.J. Griesbach, as we have already seen, not only produced the first *Synopsis* but also produced the first real solution to the Synoptic

---

likelihood, that the Gospels were primarily designed to be read aloud to groups of people, in which case the reference here to 'the reader' is a direct address to the one reading aloud to the people, perhaps encouraging him or her to place special stress on this part of the text. The point about these being texts with a *literary* relationship of course remains even if these texts were read aloud. We are still talking about text to text relationship rather than about oral tradition to text relationship.

Problem, the solution that bears his name[6] and which has recently been revived, as we will see in more detail later on. It is not his theory, though, that has dominated the discipline. Rather, the history of the study of the Synoptic Problem is largely identical with the history of the emergence of what came to be the dominant hypothesis, the Two-Source Theory.

a. *The Two-Source Theory*
The Two-Source Theory has two facets: the Priority of Mark and the Q hypothesis. It solves the Synoptic Problem by postulating independent use of Mark's Gospel by both Matthew and Luke, who are also held to have had independent access to a now lost document that scholars call 'Q'. Roughly speaking, Matthew and Luke are dependent on Mark in all those passages where there is agreement between Matthew, Mark and Luke; and they are dependent on Q in all those passages where there is agreement between just Matthew and Luke. It is represented diagrammatically like this:

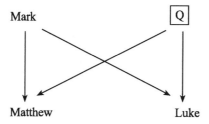

Fig. 1. *The Two-Source Theory*

The two facets of this theory, Markan Priority and Q, both emerged relatively early in the history of the discipline. That is, they were already well established by the beginning of the twentieth century. Although Markan Priority is really the older of the two, advocated already at the end of the eighteenth century, Q was well established by the end of the nineteenth century and often at this stage called 'Logia' (Sayings), in German *Logienquelle* (Sayings Source). Indeed the term

---

6.   See n. 2 above. But to complicate matters, it is now thought that the 'Gries-bach Theory' was actually conceived first by Henry Owen, *Observations on the Four Gospels* (London: T. Payne, 1764).

'Q' is thought to have originated as the first letter of the German word *Quelle*, meaning source.[7]

Right down to the present, this has remained the most popular way to solve the Synoptic Problem. It has been finely tuned, has been given many variations, and has been challenged from many quarters, but this basic two-pronged hypothesis has remained fairly effectively intact. In Germany it is still very much what one might call 'critical orthodoxy'. Famously, in the mid 1960s, one biblical critic spoke about abandoning use of the term 'hypothesis' to describe it altogether. 'We can in fact regard it as an assured finding', he said.[8]

Summary

- The *Two-Source Theory* is the most popular way of solving the Synoptic Problem, especially among German scholars
- According to the Two-Source Theory, Matthew and Luke independently used two sources, *Mark* and an hypothetical source called *Q*.

b. *The Farrer Theory*

The Two-Source Theory has had a rougher ride, though, in Great Britain and the United States. In Great Britain a steady challenge has been mounted over the last half century or so from those who, while accepting Markan Priority, are doubtful about Q. For this group, Luke reads not only Mark but also Matthew:

7.   Those interested in pursuing the history of the investigation of the problem in more detail might find W.G. Kümmel, *Introduction to the New Testament* (ET; London: SCM Press, 1966), pp. 37-42, a good starting-point. For the pre-history of the Synoptic Problem broadly conceived, see David L. Dungan, *A History of the Synoptic Problem: The Canon, the Text, the Composition and the Interpretation of the Gospels* (New York: Doubleday, 1999).

8.   Willi Marxsen, *Introduction to the New Testament: An Approach to its Problems* (ET; Oxford: Basil Blackwell, 1968), p. 118.

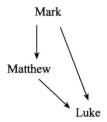

Fig. 2. *The Farrer Theory*

This movement began with the Oxford scholar Austin Farrer, whose seminal article 'On Dispensing with Q' appeared in 1955.[9] Farrer claims that if it can be shown to be plausible that Luke knew Matthew as well as Mark, then the Q theory becomes superfluous to requirements—one can 'dispense' with Q. But Farrer only wrote the one article on this topic. Michael Goulder, originally a pupil of Austin Farrer, has become the key advocate for this theory, devoting two books and many articles to arguing the case with vigour.[10] Over the years, the theory has gathered a handful of prominent supporters. In Great Britain it is this thesis that has become the Two-Source Theory's greatest rival.

c. *The Griesbach Theory*

In the United States, the main contemporary challenger to the Two-Source Theory is currently the Griesbach Theory, already mentioned, which was revived by William Farmer in his book *The Synoptic Problem* in 1964.[11] This theory dispenses with *both* facets of the Two-Source Theory, not only Q but also Markan Priority. Mark therefore comes third and uses both Matthew, written first, and Luke, who read Matthew. It might be represented diagrammatically like this:

9.   Austin Farrer, 'On Dispensing With Q', in D.E. Nineham (ed.), *Studies in the Gospels: Essays in Memory of R.H. Lightfoot* (Oxford: Basil Blackwell, 1955), pp. 55-88 (reproduced on-line at Mark Goodacre [ed.], *The Case Against Q: A Synoptic Problem Web Site, http://NTGateway.com/Q*).

10. Michael D. Goulder, *Midrash and Lection in Matthew* (London: SPCK, 1974) and *Luke: A New Paradigm* (JSNTSup, 20; Sheffield: Sheffield Academic Press, 1989). For further bibliography on the Farrer Theory, see Goodacre, *The Case Against Q* (previous note).

11. W.R. Farmer, *The Synoptic Problem: A Critical Analysis* (Macon, GA: Mercer University Press, 2nd edn, 1976).

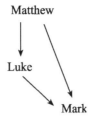

Fig. 3. *The Griesbach Theory*

A weighty and vocal minority continue to advocate this hypothesis with energy and application.

Summary

- The two most important rivals to the Two-Source Theory are the *Farrer Theory* and the *Griesbach Theory*.
- *The Farrer Theory* advocates Markan Priority but dispenses with Q by postulating Luke's knowledge of Matthew as well as Mark.
- *The Griesbach Theory* advocates neither Markan Priority nor Q, but postulates Matthean Priority, Luke's use of Matthew and Mark's use of both.

d. *The Contemporary Situation*

It is worth stressing, though, that however vocal the minorities are that present these alternative hypotheses, these do nevertheless remain minority theories. Even in Great Britain and the United States, where the Synoptic Problem is still often openly discussed, the Two-Source Theory is accepted without question by the vast majority of scholars in the discipline. If one were to take off the shelf at random almost any contemporary book on the Gospels, that book is likely to assume the correctness of the Two-Source Theory. It is a matter that is simply taken for granted in much of the scholarship, a mind set that does not often get suspended, even for a moment.

There is actually an interesting phenomenon in contemporary Gospel scholarship, a division between those who have written books and articles directly dealing with the Synoptic Problem and those who have not. Among those who might be called experts on the Synoptic

Problem, there is a variety of opinion—a good proportion believe in the Two-Source Theory but an equally high proportion question at least some aspect of it. On the other hand, among those who write books on the Gospels not dealing directly with the Synoptic Problem, there tends to be a kind of blithe confidence, almost a complacency over the correctness of the Two-Source Theory. It is a interesting state of affairs. It will be exciting to see whether in this new century the dissenting voices will be stilled by the weight of an overwhelming consensus opinion, or whether the doubters' views will steadily impinge on, and gradually transform their opponents' determined stance.

Summary

- The vast majority of New Testament scholars accept the Two-Source Theory.
- Among experts on the Synoptic Problem, the Two-Source Theory is still controversial.

5. *Why Study the Synoptic Problem?*

The thought that this kind of question will continue to rage on for many years may of course fill some with horror. Surely, after all this time, a final solution ought to have been settled upon? Or, since a solution that satisfies everyone has not been found, it might be said that it is time to surrender the hope of achieving a complete consensus and to devote one's labour to more profitable enterprises. But the Synoptic Problem will not go away. It continues to exert a fascination and an importance like nothing else in biblical studies. One might say that there are, broadly, four reasons—historical, theological, cultural and literary— that make the study of the Synoptic Problem worthwhile.

a. *History*

One of the main reasons for the continued interest is undoubtedly the matter of historical enquiry. For most New Testament scholars, in spite of the rise of new, sometimes profitable ways of reading texts, historical questions remain important and interesting. How historically accurate are our Gospels? Is one more reliable or authentic than any of the others? Is there any way of locating traditions within the Gospels that may represent a more dependable strand than others? Questions like this, whether consciously or otherwise, have always been at the heart of study of the Synoptic Problem.

Many have used the Synoptic Problem as a means to help in the quest of the historical Jesus. First one finds the most reliable sources and then one uses them to reconstruct Jesus' life. This has been particularly the case in relation to the Two-Source Theory. In much of the older scholarship, for example, Mark's Gospel was stressed as a valuable, primitive historical source. More recently, in some American scholarship there has been a great stress on Q as the most primitive 'lost gospel', reconstructions of which provide an especially valuable source of information on the historical Jesus.

It does need to be noticed, though, that there are difficulties with this quest. Its basic assumption, that earliest is best, is open to challenge. A truer word may be spoken by one who long post-dates the events he or she is describing than by one who writes closer to those same events. Further, given the variety of opinion on the Synoptic Problem, one is really walking across a minefield if one relies on one particular theory, whether the Two-Source Theory or another, in reconstructing the life of the historical Jesus. Some recent studies on Jesus thus avoid committing themselves on synoptic theories altogether.

Nevertheless, doing historical study of the New Testament period is not simply a matter of looking at the historical Jesus. There are other historical questions that are interesting. The issue of whether or not Mark preceded Matthew is itself a fascinating question. Let us illustrate this with another example, an example that, incidentally, illustrates nicely the way in which different evangelists produce different information on the same character—all say that the man in this story is rich, Matthew alone says that he is young and Luke alone says that he is a ruler:

Matthew 19.16-17	*Mark 10.17-18*	*Luke 18.18-19*
And behold, one having approached him said, 'Teacher, what *good* shall I do in order that I might have eternal life?' And he said to him, 'Why do	And as he was setting out on the way, one having run and knelt before him asked him, '*Good* teacher, what shall I do in order that I might inherit eternal life? And Jesus said to him, 'Why do you	And a certain ruler asked him, '*Good* teacher, what having done shall I inherit eternal life?' And Jesus said to him, 'Why do you

| you ask me concerning *good?* One there is who is good'. | call me *good?* No-one is good except God alone'. | call me *good?* No-one is good except God alone'. |

What is interesting is the position of the first 'good' in Matthew on the one hand and Mark and Luke on the other. Most believe that Matthew is using Mark here and that he is troubled by the implication of the question 'Why do you call me good?' Matthew therefore re-phrases (very slightly) in such a way as to change the question and avoid the difficult implication that Jesus might be admitting to not being wholly 'good'. Here, perhaps, we witness an interesting moment in the development of Christian doctrine, for in the change from the unembarrassed brashness of Mark to the more measured, reverential Matthew, we see perceptions of Jesus' identity subtly changing.[12]

But then if one believes instead in Matthaean Priority, the matter is reversed—Mark (or Luke and then Mark) makes the earlier, reverential Matthew more 'gritty' and realistic. The move from one form of words to another, though perhaps more surprising, remains just as interesting. And there are many such striking differences between the Synoptics. Let us take another illustration:

Matthew 8.25-26	*Mark 4.38-39*	*Luke 8.24-25*
And the disciples, having approached him, awoke him saying, 'Lord, save! We are perishing!' * Then, having got up, he rebuked the winds and the sea,	And they awake him and say to him, 'Teacher, do you not care that we are perishing?' And having awoken, he rebuked the wind and said to the sea, 'Be silent! Be muzzled!' And the wind	And having approached him they awoke him saying, 'Master Master, we are perishing!' And having awoken, he rebuked the wind and the raging of the water. And they
and there was a great calm'. *And he says to them, 'Why are you afraid, ye of little faith?'*	ceased, and there was a great calm. And he said to them, 'Why are you so afraid? Have you still no faith?'	ceased, and there was a calm. And he said to them, 'Where is your faith?'

12. For an excellent discussion of these issues, see Peter Head, *Christology and the Synoptic Problem: An Argument for Markan Priority* (SNTSMS, 94; Cambridge: Cambridge University Press, 1997).

One cannot help noticing a contrast here between Mark on the one hand and Matthew and Luke on the other. Mark's Jesus shows no respect for the disciples: 'Have you still no faith?' And the disciples, apparently, show no respect for Jesus: 'Do you not care...?' In both Matthew and Luke there is more reverence. In Matthew they have 'little faith', not none, and in Luke the question is, 'Where is your faith?', as if this is but a temporary lapse. Likewise, in neither Matthew nor Luke do they ask the insulting question, 'Do you not care...?'

Again, then, one finds significant differences revealed as soon as parallel accounts are placed in Synopsis. It is seeing the accounts in parallel that focuses important issues. And one inevitably finds oneself asking interesting historical questions: Why are Matthew and Luke more reverential in their portrait of Jesus? Why does Mark apparently paint the disciples of Jesus in such a negative light?

Summary

- Scholars use the Synoptic Problem in an attempt to solve historical puzzles.
- The Two-Source Theory is sometimes used to help in the quest of the historical Jesus.
- The Synoptic Problem asks interesting historical questions about the Gospels and their place in the development of Christianity.

b. *Theology*

Such questions are not, of course, only of historical interest, for clearly they have important theological dimensions. Indeed synoptic study, by accentuating the differences between the Gospels, can help to sharpen important theological questions. To follow on from the above examples, what does synoptic study tell us about shades of first-century Christology? What does it tell us about the way the disciples, some of whom became the leaders of the Church, were viewed?

The way in which the Synoptic Problem can help to focus theological issues might be illustrated from a famous synoptic comparison. The institution of the Eucharist is found not only in the Synoptics but also in Paul (1 Cor. 11). This is an excerpt:

Matthew 26.27-28	Mark 14.23-24	Luke 22.20	1 Corinthians 11.25
And after he had taken the cup and given thanks, he gave it to them saying, 'Drink from it, all.	And after he had taken the cup and given thanks, he gave it to them and they all drank from it. And he said to them,	And likewise (he took) the cup after supper, saying,	And likewise (he took) the cup after supper, saying,
For this is my blood of the covenant which is shed for many *for the forgiveness of sins'*.	'This is my blood of the covenant which is shed for many'.	'This cup is the *new* covenant in my blood, which is shed for you'.	'This cup is the *new* covenant in my blood. Do this, as often as you drink, in my memory'.

There is a complex web of interrelated material here, perhaps largely because we are dealing with a liturgical text, something that has been repeated over and over again, with variations, in different locations, from the thirties onwards. The comparison between the four accounts draws attention to several interesting theological points. Matthew alone has 'for the forgiveness of sins'. Luke and Paul alone have 'new covenant' and Paul alone here has 'in my memory'. It is the analysis of this kind of passage, and the attempt to explain both the similarities and the differences, that gives the study of the Synoptic Problem one of its great attractions.

At the very least, one notices that there is not one unanimous picture of 'the Eucharist' or 'Christology' in early Christianity. The agreements and disagreements draw attention to the fact that there was a dialogue going on in the first century, a dialogue that spawned the controversies of future years, and which, more importantly, can help us to focus some of our own theological questions.

Thus the use of the Synopsis is potentially a powerful tool for aiding proper theological reflection. The harmonizing of texts can be a damaging means of interweaving subtle personal agendas into the rephrasing of disparate elements—and robbing the texts of their vitality. What is exciting about studying texts in Synopsis is the matter of stressing the differences between them, and asking how one might react theologically to them.

Summary

- The Synoptic Problem draws attention to historical questions that in turn give rise to theological questions.
- The Synoptic Problem, by drawing attention to differences between parallel texts, can stimulate theological reflection.

c. *Cultural Factors*

The difficulty with such perspectives, however, is that they will appear somewhat old-fashioned to the reader interested in contemporary, post-modern ways of reading the Gospels. Recent years have seen the rise, for example, of reader-response criticism, which tends to place stress on the recipient of the text (the contemporary reader) rather than the originator of the text (the author). Does the Synoptic Problem have anything to offer to such readers? Or is it only for those still stuck in the antiquated enterprise of doing historical-critical work on the New Testament?

The answer to this question is that *as traditionally defined*, the Synoptic Problem has very little to offer to those interested in contemporary approaches. In other words, those writing on the Synoptic Problem tend to focus on historical-critical questions. For them the goal is to provide a perfect solution to the problem of who wrote first, who copied from whom, and whether there are any lost documents.

But this need not remain the status quo. Contemporary, culturally relevant study of the Synoptic Problem may take off in other directions, and it is may be that this is where the future of the discipline lies. It is worth noting, for example, that, in spite of the proliferation of narra-tive-critical, reader-response and literary-critical readings of each of our Gospels, at present there is little that attempts to apply such meth-ods to parallel texts in Synopsis. This is a weakness of the current scene, in which scholars have become so besotted with responding to texts in isolation from one another that they have forgotten that the texts have, and have always been perceived as having, an intimate interrela-tionship.

Of course, at this stage it is difficult to know what study of the Synoptic Problem that is sympathetic to contemporary methodologies might look like. For those interested in the way that the Bible is used in culture one obvious starting point might be the realization with which we began this chapter, that the popular perception of the Gospels still involves a tendency towards the harmonizing of different texts. The writing of harmonies of the Gospels did not, after all, die a death as soon as Griesbach produced the first Synopsis. On the contrary, one only needs a passing acquaintance with contemporary representations of 'the Jesus story' to notice that harmonizing is alive and well. In such circumstances, there is a wealth of research waiting to be done on the way in which Jesus films, for example, have combined and conflated synoptic (and Johannine) data, study that will no doubt prove not only to be generated by awareness of the Synoptic Problem, but which may also, in turn, shed fresh light on it.

The application of newer approaches to the Synoptic Problem may be the best hope for its future, particularly if we are to avoid the endless repetition of some mistakes, going round in the same circles, investigating the same texts in the same way. This is a challenge for the new century, and we will return to the question in the Conclusion below.

Summary

- Scholars of the Synoptic Problem rarely engage with new methods of reading the Gospels, like *narrative-criticism*.
- The application of contemporary critical methods to the Synoptic Problem is potentially exciting and challenging.

d. *The Literary Puzzle*

But if the historical dimension of the Synoptic Problem is what has exercised the minds of scholars for the last two hundred years, it is worth noting that this study is worth doing for its own sake, and needs no other reason than that it is enormously good fun. In other words, the Synoptic Problem is an intriguing phenomenon for study in its own right—and it is a form of study that needs no apology. For in the Synoptic Problem one has, without doubt, one of the most fascinating literary puzzles in world history. There are plenty of examples in literature from all cultures of different accounts of similar events, of complex interweaving of sources and of uncertainties about origin and dependence. Indeed, there are good examples of these phenomena elsewhere in the Bible, as in the overlap in the Old Testament between Kings and Chronicles, or between Isaiah 36–39 and 2 Kings 18–20.

Yet there is nothing to match the Synoptic Problem for the sheer con-
tours, variations, depths and shape of the discipline. Those who think
that they have mastered it regularly discover fresh complications. Those
who believe that they can explain all the data then come across an
argument that appears more plausible than their own.

Summary

- Above all, the Synoptic Problem is interesting in its own right
  as a fascinating literary enigma.

---

6. *Summary and Conclusion*

At the end of each chapter in this book there is a summary in which all
the most important elements in the discussion will be underlined. So
far, we have discovered the following:

(a) The popular way to read the Gospels has been to *harmonize*
     them with one another. However, for the last two hundred
     years, Gospel harmonies have been rivalled by *Synopses* of
     the Gospels, in which the Gospels are placed side by side for
     the purposes of careful comparison.
     - The Synopsis gives birth to the term *Synoptic Gospels*,
       Matthew, Mark and Luke. This is because there are
       extensive agreements between Matthew, Mark and
       Luke, but much less agreement between these Gospels
       and John.
     - The Synopsis also gives birth to the *Synoptic Problem*,
       an enterprise that studies the similarities and differ-
       ences among the Synoptic Gospels in a bid to find an
       explanation for their interrelationship.
(b) The dominant solution to the Synoptic Problem is the *Two-
     Source Theory*, which supposes that Matthew and Luke both
     used Mark (*the Priority of Mark*), but that they also used an
     hypothetical source, '*Q*'.
     - The two major alternatives are the *Farrer Theory*,
       which affirms Markan Priority but dispenses with Q,
       and the *Griesbach Theory*, which rejects both Markan
       Priority and Q.

(c)   Several reasons might be given for engaging in the study of the Synoptic Problem:

- *Historical*: solving the Synoptic Problem helps one to answer historical questions, questions about reliable sources of information on the historical Jesus and questions about the development of early Christianity.
- *Theological*: examining the Synoptic Problem encourages theological reflection about the interaction between the Gospel texts.
- *Contemporary*: although not currently popular, there are ways in which the Synoptic Problem might profitably interact with contemporary approaches to the New Testament, like narrative-criticism.
- *The Literary Puzzle*: the Synoptic Problem is probably the most fascinating literary enigma of all time.

Let us, then, having entered the maze, begin to explore it. Before doing this, though, readers should be warned. They should not be under any illusions. Study of the Synoptic Problem sometimes feels like walking through a maze that is in a constant state of change. Workers are busy constructing new walls even as one is finding the way through. But despite this, entering the maze is more than worthwhile. It is a challenging yet rewarding academic puzzle. And that this most fascinating of literary enigmas should happen to concern accounts of one of the most important historical figures ever to have lived gives the Synoptic Problem, to say the least, an addesd thrilling dimension.

Chapter 2

EXPLORING THE MAZE: THE DATA

1. *Introduction*

Before looking any further at attempts to solve the Synoptic Problem, it is essential to be clear about the basic data. What kind of material does one find in the Synoptic Gospels? Is it easily classifiable? Is there a great deal of variety? Is it impossibly complex? The reader anxious over such questions will be glad to hear the good news that the majority of the material is easily classified into four major types, each of which is fairly self-explanatory. The types of material tend to be called *Triple Tradition*, *Double Tradition*, *Special Matthew* and *Special Luke*. There are some complications, and we will come to these in due course, but for the time being it is important to grasp that the vast majority of material in the Synoptics is easily classified into one of these four types. In a moment we will begin to take each kind of material in turn. But first, let me recommend a task to all newcomers to the Synoptic Problem, a task that will help familiarize you with the Synopsis, introducing you to the different kinds of agreement and disagreement among them.

2. *Task: Colouring the Synopsis*

In order to do this task, you need a Synopsis of the Gospels[1] and some coloured pencils or crayons. If you cannot get hold of a Synopsis

1. If you can read Greek there are essentially two choices for Synopses of the Gospels: Albert Huck, *Synopsis of the First Three Gospels* (fundamentally revised by Heinrich Greeven; Tübingen: J.C.B. Mohr [Paul Siebeck], 13th edn, 1981)—this is known as 'Huck–Greeven'; or Kurt Aland, *Synopsis Quattuor Evangeliorum* (Stuttgart: Deutsche Bibelgesellschaft, 15th edn, 1996, 1997). For those without Greek, I recommend either K. Aland (ed.), *Synopsis of the Four Gospels* (English; Stuttgart: Deutsche Bibelgesellschaft, 1985) or Burton H. Throckmorton, Jr, *Gospel*

straight away, try photocopying some of the sample Synopses in this book, or, if you have access to the Internet, you can print sample Synopses from there. Indeed, if you have access to the Internet, you will also be able to look at some samples of coloured Synopsis on this book's web site.[2]

Find a parallel passage, print or photocopy it and look at similarities and differences between Matthew, Mark and Luke. You might like to begin straight away on the passages we will be using as examples in this chapter. These are:

Mt. 9.9//Mk 2.14//Lk. 5.27 (Levi)
Mt. 3.7-10//Lk. 3.7-9 (John the Baptist's Preaching)
Mt. 7.3-5//Lk. 6.41-43 (Log and Speck)
Mt. 3.13-17//Mk 1.9-11//Lk. 3.21-22 (Baptism)
Mt. 14.34-36//Mk 6.53-56 (Healing at Gennesaret)
Mk 12.41-44//Lk. 21.1-4 (Widow's Mite)
Mt. 13.31-32//Mk 4.30-32//Lk. 13.18-19 (Mustard Seed)

Now begin colouring. Use one colour for words found only in Matthew, one colour for words found only in Mark and one colour for words found only in Luke. You should use one colour for words found in both Matthew and Luke but not in Mark, one colour for words found in Mark and Luke but not in Matthew, one colour for words found in Matthew and Luke but not in Mark, and one colour for words found in all three.

Different individuals have different tastes and so use different schemes, but the one that I have found most useful in several years of intensive Synopsis colouring is based on the three primary colours, one for each Synoptist, and the secondary colours that arise from combining them. I strongly recommend that you use this system in your colouring of the Synopsis, not least because I will illustrate how the different kinds of data appear in the rest of this chapter by drawing attention to these colours, but also because it is a system that anyone who has done any elementary mixing of paint will be familiar with:

Matthew: *blue*
Mark: *red*
Luke: *yellow*

Parallels: A Comparison of the Synoptic Gospels (Nashville, TN: Thomas Nelson, 1993).
2.   http://www.ntgateway.com/maze.

Matthew + Mark: *purple* [i.e. blue + red]
Matthew + Luke: *green* [i.e. blue + yellow]
Mark + Luke: *orange* [i.e. red + yellow]

Matthew + Mark + Luke: *brown* [i.e. blue + red + yellow]

The look of your Synopsis will depend very much on which passage you have chosen to colour. And the spread of colours in each of the passages will help you to see the characteristics of each of the different kinds of material that we are now ready to discuss. So, having begun to familiarize ourselves with the Synopsis, let take a closer look at the different kinds of material we find there.

3. *Triple Tradition*

The first kind of synoptic material tends to be called *Triple Tradition* and we have already, in Chapter 1, seen several examples of it. It involves cases where a pericope is featured in all three Synoptics. Hence the Synopsis has at these points three columns—as above in the case of the Leper, the Call of Levi/Matthew (for which see also below), the Stilling of the Storm and the Rich Young Ruler.

There are many famous examples of Triple Tradition material and they include the following:

Table 1. *Triple Tradition*

Matthew	Mark	Luke	Event
8.1-4	1.40-45	5.12-16	Leper
9.1-8	2.1-12	5.17-26	Paralytic
9.9-13	2.13-17	5.27-32	Call of Levi/Matthew
9.14-17	2.18-22	5.33-39	Fasting, New Wine, Patches
12.1-8	2.23-28	6.1-5	Plucking Grain on the Sabbath
12.9-14	3.1-6	6.6-11	Man with Withered Hand
10.1-4	3.13-19	6.12-16	Choosing of the Twelve
12.46-50	3.31-35	8.19-21	Jesus' Mother and Brothers
13.1-23	4.1-20	8.4-15	Parable of the Sower
8.23-27	4.35-41	8.22-25	Calming of the Storm
8.28-34	5.1-20	8.26-39	Gerasene Demoniac
9.18-26	5.21-43	8.40-56	Jairus's Daughter and Woman
14.13-21	6.30-44	9.10-17	Feeding of Five Thousand
16.13-20	8.27-30	9.18-21	Peter's Confession
17.1-8	9.2-8	9.28-36	Transfiguration
17.14-20	9.14-29	9.37-43	Epileptic Boy

Matthew	Mark	Luke	Event
19.13-15	10.13-16	18.15-17	Little Children
19.16-30	10.17-31	18.18-30	Rich Young Ruler
20.29-34	10.46-52	18.35-43	Blind Bartimaeus
21.1-9	11.1-10	19.28-38	Triumphal Entry
21-28	11-16	20-24	Passion Narrative

This is a large body of material. It contains a substantial amount of sayings material, including the Parable of the Sower and the Parable of the Wicked Husbandmen (Mt. 21.33-46//Mk 12.1-12//Lk. 20.9-19). It also contains much narrative material—it is especially rich in healing and miracle stories (Leper; Paralytic; Bartimaeus; Feeding of the Five Thousand; Stilling of the Storm, to mention just a few).

Let us then remind ourselves of how this material appears in the Synopsis:

Matthew 9.9	Mark 2.14	Luke 5.27
And having passed on from there, Jesus saw a man	And having passed on he saw Levi son of Alphaeus	And he saw a tax-collector named Levi
seated in the tax-office, named Matthew,	seated in the tax-office,	seated in the tax-office,
and he says to him, 'Follow me'. And having arisen, he followed him.	and he says to him, 'Follow me'. And having arisen, he followed him.	and he said to him, 'Follow me'. And having left everything and having arisen, he followed him.

If you have not already done so, now is the time to colour this piece of Synopsis. This will help you to see the way in which the Synoptics agree and disagree. Most fundamentally, there is substantial agreement between all three (for example, 'seated in the tax-office'; 'Follow me'; 'having arisen, he followed him'). If you are using the colouring scheme suggested earlier, these passages will be brown. It is also the case, however, that Matthew and Mark sometimes agree together against Luke (purple). They both begin 'And having passed on', but Luke does not. Similarly, they both have 'he says to him' but Luke has 'he said'. Further, Mark and Luke agree together against Matthew on a key point of the story, naming the man Levi rather than Matthew (orange). Matthew and Luke also agree together against Mark, but less obviously—they have 'named' and omit some of the same material ('son of Alphaeus', etc.).

This general phenomenon is a key feature of the Triple Tradition—Mark is *the middle term* among the Synoptics. There is substantial agreement between all three Synoptics, some agreement between Matthew and Mark against Luke, some agreement between Mark and Luke against Matthew, but less agreement between Matthew and Luke against Mark. When the Synopsis has been coloured, the pattern contains lots of brown, some purple, some orange but little green. The pattern therefore looks like this:

MATTHEW	MARK	LUKE
MATTHEW	MARK	
	MARK	LUKE

That is to say (to repeat) that we have agreements between Matthew, Mark and Luke, between Mark and Luke alone and between Matthew and Luke alone. If you have done your colouring, you will see in Triple Tradition fair amounts of brown, purple and orange, but much less green. It is Mark, then, that tends to be the common element, the 'middle term'.

This situation is true not just in the wording but also in the arrangement of material. Triple Tradition has broadly the same order across the three Synoptics, and this order tends to be identical with Mark's order. On occasions, Luke places an incident differently. Mt. 12.46-50//Mk 3.31-35//Lk. 8.19-21 (Mother and Brothers), for example, is Triple Tradition material that occurs before the Parable of the Sower in Matthew and Mark, but a little while after it in Luke. On other occasions Matthew places an incident differently. The Healing of Jairus's Daughter and the Woman with the haemorrhage (Mt. 9.18-26//Mk 5.21-43//Lk. 8.40-56), for example, is placed just after the Question about Fasting in Matthew (9.14-17), the parallel to which comes much earlier in both Mk (2.18-22) and Luke (5.33-39).

The striking thing about Triple Tradition is, however, that it is rare for *both* Matthew *and* Luke to place the same incident differently. One thus has the following pattern in the order of Triple Tradition: either Matthew, Mark and Luke all agree, or Matthew and Mark agree together against Luke, or Mark and Luke agree together against Matthew. It is unusual to find Matthew and Luke agreeing together against Mark. In other words, Mark is also *the middle term* in the question of the order of Triple Tradition material, just as it was in the question of the wording of parallel pericopae. Again, this is the pattern:

MATTHEW	MARK	LUKE
MATTHEW	MARK	
	MARK	LUKE

A corollary of this is the most striking feature of Triple Tradition material, that if one were to isolate this material from all the rest, one would have something closely resembling a complete Gospel, and this Gospel would look similar to Mark. One finds John the Baptist, Jesus' Baptism and Temptation; the announcement of the kingdom and the call of the disciples (all Mk 1 with parallels in Mt. 3–4 and Lk. 3–4); a ministry in Galilee (Mk 1–9 with parallels in Matthew and Luke); a journey to Jerusalem (Mk 10–11 and parallels) and ministry in Jerusalem (Mk 11–13 and parallels); followed by a Passion Narrative (Mk 14–15 and parallels) and Resurrection account (Mk 16 and parallels). The same is not true of any of the other kinds of material that we will be isolating for comment below. This is therefore a feature that needs to be strongly noted. Every solution of the Synoptic Problem must take this feature of the material seriously. Indeed it is the Triple Tradition that is the necessary starting point in any investigation of the Synoptic Problem, and it will be the main subject of Chapter 3 below, on the theory of Markan Priority.

Summary

- *Triple Tradition* pericopae are those found in all three Synoptics. Here, the Synopsis will be in three columns.
- The order and wording of this material is similar across the three Synoptics.
- This means that there are substantial agreements in wording and order between Matthew, Mark and Luke, between Mark and Luke and between Mark and Matthew. There are only minor agreements between Matthew and Luke against Mark. Mark is, in other words, *the middle term*. If the colouring scheme suggested above is followed, the Synopsis will feature a good deal of brown, some purple and some orange. There is usually relatively little green.

4. *Double Tradition*

The second kind of synoptic material is found in Matthew and Luke but not in Mark. It is called 'Double Tradition' or sometimes 'Q material', the latter term used without necessarily prejudicing the issue of the origin of the material. We have encountered this once already, above, when looking at the preaching of John the Baptist. The Synopsis here has two columns and, let us remind ourselves, looks like this:

Matthew 3.7-10	Luke 3.7-9
'Offspring of vipers! Who warned you to flee from the coming wrath? Bear fruit therefore worthy of repentance and do not *presume* to say in yourselves, "We have Abraham as father"; for I say to you that God is able from these stones to raise up children to Abraham. Already the axe is laid at the root of the trees; for every tree not producing good fruit is cut down and cast into the fire'.	'Offspring of vipers! Who warned you to flee from the coming wrath? Bear fruit therefore worthy of repentance and do not *begin* to say in yourselves, "We have Abraham as father"; for I say to you that God is able from these stones to raise up children to Abraham. Already the axe is laid at the root of the trees; for every tree not producing good fruit is cut down and cast into the fire'.

Don't forget to photocopy or print out this passage and colour it.

You will see a striking difference in your colours from the colours found in Triple Tradition passages above. Where there there was very little green, here we have the opposite—almost entirely green. This is a typical example of Double Tradition material. Like most of 'Q', it is not narrative but sayings. The Double Tradition overall is made up of somewhere between 200 and 250 verses of such sayings material, usually, of course, Jesus' own speech. Often the material is as close in agreement as the example here—there is nothing exceptional about close agreement. Take, for example, this excerpt from the Sermon on the Mount/Plain:

Matthew 7.3-5	Luke 6.41-43
And why do you see the speck that is in your brother's eye, but the log which is in your eye you do not consider? Or how can you say to your brother,	And why do you see the speck that is in your brother's eye, but the log which is in your own eye you do not consider? How are you able to say to your brother, 'Brother,
'Allow me to take out the speck from your eye', and behold the log in your eye! Hypocrites! First take the log out of your eye, and then you will be able to see to take out the speck from your brother's eye.	allow me to take the speck that is in your eye', when you yourself do not see the log in your eye! Hypocrites! First take the log out of your eye, and then you will be able to see to take out the speck from your brother's eye.

There are little variations between the accounts—Luke has a characteristic 'Brother...' and Matthew a characteristic 'behold', but overall the agreement is very close. Again, the colour most used here will be green.

These are some of the most famous Double Tradition pericopae:

Table 2. *Double Tradition*

Matthew	Luke	Event
5-7	6.20-49	Sermon on the Mount/Plain
8.5-13	7.1-10	Centurion's Servant
11.2-19	7.18-35	Messengers from John the Baptist
11.20-24	10.12-15	Woes on the Cities of Galilee
11.25-27	10.21-22	Jesus' Thanksgiving to the Father
12.43-45	11.24-26	Return of the Evil Spirit
13.33	13.20-21	Parable of the Leaven
18.10-14	15.3-7	Parable of the Lost Sheep

Matthew	Luke	Event
22.1-14	14.15-24	Parable of the Marriage Feast/Great Supper
25.14-30	19.11-27	Parable of the Talents/Pounds
23.1-36	11.37-54	Discourse Against Scribes (Lawyers) and Pharisees
23.37-39	13.34-35	Lament Over Jerusalem
24.45-51	12.39-46	Parable of the Faithful and Wise Servant

Several features of interest are evident from a glance at this table. First, one will see that, although Double Tradition material is largely sayings material, there are apparent exceptions, the most obvious of which are the Centurion's Servant (or, more accurately, the Centurion's Boy—only Luke definitely identifies him as a servant) and the Messengers from John the Baptist. Nevertheless, although they have a narrative setting, even these pericopae are mainly made up of sayings.

Another matter of interest here is the range of agreement between Matthew and Luke. We saw above that often agreement is very close in the Double Tradition, illustrated by the examples of the Preaching of John the Baptist and the Log and the Speck. However, in the case of the Parable of the Talents/Pounds, or the Parable of the Marriage Feast/Great Supper, the agreement is much more slight—indeed, one even has to give the parallel accounts different names in each Gospel.

Further, one quickly notices a major difference between this material and the Triple Tradition. For, whereas in that material there is a substantial similarity in the order of pericopae between the three Synoptics, here there is major variation. While there are some similarities in order—such as the placing of the Centurion's Servant just after the Sermon on the Mount/Plain (with the Leper intervening in Mt. 8.1-4)—there are big differences too. The Parable of the Faithful and Wise Servant occurs roughly halfway through Luke's Gospel, in ch. 12, but it occurs towards the end of Matthew's, in ch. 24. Likewise, there are major differences over the positioning of the Lament over Jerusalem (Mt. 23.37-39//Lk. 13.34-35), the Discourse against the Scribes and the Pharisees (Mt. 23.1-36//Lk. 11.37-54) and the Parable of the Wedding Feast/Great Supper (Mt. 22.1-14//Lk. 14.15-24). Much, too, of the material found in Matthew's Sermon on the Mount is located differently in Luke—the passage on Care and Anxiety, for example ('Consider the lilies…') is in the middle of Matthew's Sermon (ch. 6) but much later on in Luke (12.22-34). Similarly, the Lord's Prayer, also in Matthew 6, is found at the beginning of Luke 11.

The phenomenon of order is, as I have already hinted, one of the key areas for the study of the Synoptic Problem. Whole books have been devoted to this topic alone.[3] Much of the discussion revolves around the matter of the Double Tradition and the fact that it seems to be placed so differently in Matthew and Luke. The problem becomes particularly intense when one asks about the placement of the Double Tradition *in relation to* the placement of the Triple Tradition in Matthew and Luke. The relationship between the Triple Tradition and the Double Tradition is something that the Two-Source Theory in particular attempts to address directly—and we will look at this issue in more detail in due course.

Summary

- *Double Tradition* pericopae are those found in Matthew and Luke alone. Here, the Synopsis will be in two columns.
- There are about 200 verses of Double Tradition, most of which is made up of sayings material, but some of which is narrative.
- The wording of this material is very similar in Matthew and Luke. If one has coloured the Synopsis, there will be lots of green in these passages.
- Although there are some similarities, overall the order of this material is different in Matthew and Luke.

5. *Special Matthew*

The third kind of synoptic material is even more obviously self-explanatory than is Triple Tradition or Double Tradition. 'Special Matthew', or 'M' material, is that which is unique to Matthew among the Gospels. Although this material is an important aspect of the Synoptic Problem, it is not, strictly speaking 'synoptic', for here there are of course no columns, and the Synopsis will revert to printing the text like that of a normal book. There is no need to colour these M passages, but if you do you will simply have lots of the colour blue.

3. See the excellent study by David J. Neville, *Arguments from Order in Synoptic Source Criticism: A History and Critique* (New Gospel Studies, 7; Macon, GA: Mercer University Press, 1994).

Like all other strands of material, Special Matthew features some famous pericopae. This is a list of the most well-known:

Table 3. *Special Matthew (M)*

Matthew	Event
Mt. 1.1-17, though cf. Lk. 3.23-38	Genealogy
Mt. 1–2, though cf. Lk. 1–2	Birth Narratives
Mt. 11.28-30	'Come to me all those who labour…'
Mt. 13.24-30, 36-43; but cf. Mk 4.26-9	Parable of the Tares and its Interpretation
Mt. 13.44-46	Parables of Hidden Treasure and the Pearl
Mt. 13.47-50	Parable of the Drag-net
Mt. 17.24-27	Coin in the Fish's Mouth
Mt. 18.23-35	Parable of the Unmerciful Servant
Mt. 20.1-16	Parable of the Labourers in the Vineyard
Mt. 21.28-32	Parable of the Two Sons
Mt. 25.1-13; but cf. Lk. 12.35-36	Parable of the Ten Virgins
Mt. 25.31-46	Sheep and the Goats
Mt. 27.3-10	Death of Judas
Mt. 27.62-66	Guard at the Tomb
Mt. 28.9-10	Appearance to the Women
Mt. 28.11-15	Bribing of the Soldiers
Mt. 28.16-20	Great Commission

It should perhaps be added that some of the Sermon on the Mount (Mt. 5–7) constitutes M material, especially the first half of ch. 6. One should also note that it is often difficult to distinguish between what might be called M material and what might be regarded simply as fuller versions of Triple Tradition pericopae. In the baptism of Jesus by John, for example, there are two verses of material that appear only in Matthew (3.14-15) and not in the parallel accounts in Mark (1.9-11) and Luke (3.21-22). Here the Synopsis will look like this:

Matthew 3.13-17	Mark 1.9-11	Luke 3.21-22
Then Jesus came from Galilee to the Jordan to John to be baptized by him. But John prevented	And it came to pass in those days that Jesus came from Nazareth in Galilee	And it came to pass that while all the people were being baptized, Jesus also

him, saying, 'I need to be baptized by you, and yet you come to me?' And Jesus answered him, 'Let it be so now; for thus it is fitting for us to fulfil all righteousness'. Then he allowed him.		
And when Jesus had been baptized,	And was baptized in the Jordan by John. And immediately,	having been baptized was praying, and
he arose immediately from the water; and behold, the heavens were opened to him...	having arisen from the water, he saw the heavens torn apart...	the heaven was opened...

Two whole verses have no parallel in either Mark or Luke, so they are, in this sense, Special Matthew—they are unique to his Gospel. On the other hand, though, the verses only make sense in the narrative context provided by Triple Tradition material, that is, the surrounding verses that are paralleled in both Mark and Luke. Much of the special material is like this—unique to Matthew yet couched in a Triple Tradition narrative context—compare, for example, the following passages:

Table 4. *Special Matthew in Triple Tradition Contexts*

Matthew	Event
14.28-31	Peter's attempt to walk on the water
16.17-19	Commendation of Peter
21.14-16	Healing and children's praise in the temple
27.19	Pilate's wife's dream
27.52-53	Graves opening at Jesus' death

This feature is another one that needs to be taken into account in attempts to solve the Synoptic Problem. The kinds of questions that inevitably arise are: has Matthew added these verses to an already existing account in Mark (or Luke, or both), or have these verses been omitted from the account by Mark (or Luke, or both)?

It is worth noting one or two characteristics of the special material. Like Double Tradition, it is rich in sayings material, especially parables. There is some narrative but it is usually said that it tends towards a more blatantly 'legendary' character than the bulk of narrative material elsewhere in the Synoptics—the coin in the fish's mouth, for example, or the characters rising from the dead at Jesus' death in Jerusalem.

Summary

- *Special Matthew* pericopae are those found only in Matthew.
- Some Special Matthew material is intimately connected with the Triple Tradition contexts in which it is embedded.
- Some Special Matthew material is said to have a 'legendary' character.

6. *Special Luke*

There is, then, a good amount of material unique to Matthew. There is a greater bulk of material, however, that is unique to Luke. This is known as Special Luke or 'L' material. The reader will be familiar with much of this material—it is a favourite with preachers and it is the mainstay of many a school assembly. These are the most prominent of its pericopae:

Table 5. *Special Luke (L)*

Luke	Event
1-2; but cf. Mt. 1-2	Birth Narratives
2.41-52	Jesus as a boy in the Temple
3.23-38; but cf. Mt. 1.1-19	Genealogy of Jesus
7.11-17	Raising of the Widow of Nain's Son
8.1-3	Ministering Women
9.51-56	Samaritan Villages
10.17-20	Return of the Seventy-Two
10.29-37	Parable of the Good Samaritan
10.38-42	Martha and Mary
11.5-8	Parable of the Friend at Midnight
11.27-28	Blessedness of Jesus' Mother
12.13-21	Parable of the Rich Fool
13.1-5	Tower of Siloam
13.6-9	Parable of the Fig Tree
13.10-17	Healing of the Bent Woman
14.1-6	Healing of the Man with Dropsy

Luke	Event
14.7-14	Invitations to Feasts and Dinners
15.8-10	Parable of the Lost Coin
15.11-32	Parable of the Prodigal Son
16.19-31	Parable of Dives and Lazarus
17.7-10	Parable of the Servant of All Work
17.11-19	Healing of Ten Lepers
18.1-8	Parable of the Unjust Judge
18.9-14	Parable of the Pharisee and the Tax-Collector
19.1-10	Zacchaeus
22.35-38	Two Swords
23.6-12	Trial before Herod
24.13-35	Road to Emmaus
24.36-49	Appearance of Jesus in Jerusalem

L material shares one of the complications that was a feature of the M material—sometimes, though less often than in Matthew, it appears in a Triple Tradition narrative context, for example the discourse for 'the daughters of Jerusalem' when Jesus is on the way to the cross (Lk. 23.27-32), or the conversation with the two thieves when Jesus is on the cross (Lk. 23.40-43).

L material has an extra complication shared hardly at all by M. It is sometimes difficult to judge whether one should ascribe a piece to L or whether one should call it a different version of Triple Tradition material. The key examples of this are in the following table:

Table 6. *L Material Similar to Matthew and Mark*

Luke	Similarity	Event
4.16-30	Similar to Mt. 13.53-58//Mk 6.1-6a	Rejection at Nazareth
5.1-11	Similar to Mt. 4.18-22//Mk 1.16-20; John 21.1-11	Call of the first disciples
7.36-50	Similar to Mt. 26.6-13//Mk 14.3-9; John 12.1-8	Woman who anoints Jesus

In each case the incident is placed differently from its (partial) parallel in Matthew and Mark and in each case the account is a much fuller one. Further, on two of the occasions (Call, Anointing), there are interesting parallels too in the Gospel of John.

It may not have escaped the reader's notice that much of Luke's special material is parable material, and that many of the most famous parables are here—the Good Samaritan, the Prodigal Son, Dives and Lazarus, the Pharisee and the Publican, the Unjust Judge, the Friend at Midnight, the Rich Fool. Furthermore, some of the non-parable material is equally as rich in its colour as are the parables—it is here that one finds some of the most three-dimensional, human touches in the Gospels—the Ten Lepers, where one returns thankful; the Widow of Nain, whose only son is brought to life; Martha and Mary, where Mary is commended for listening at Jesus' feet; and the Road to Emmaus, in which the two travellers recognize their travelling companion when he breaks bread with them.

Summary

- *Special Luke* pericopae are those found only in Luke.
- Some Special Luke material is similar to pericopae in Mark.
- Special Luke contains many of the best-known materials in the Gospels (e.g. Road to Emmaus) and it is rich in parables (e.g. Good Samaritan and the Prodigal Son).

---

7. *Summary and Complications*

It is important but straightforward to grasp the data set out thus far. Having opened a Synopsis, readers should ask themselves what kind of material is in front of them. Is it Triple Tradition? If so it will appear in three columns, Matthew, Mark and Luke. Is it Double Tradition? If so it will appear in two columns, Matthew and Luke. Is it Special Matthew? If so it will appear only in Matthew. Is it Special Luke? If so it will appear only in Luke.

These kinds of material make up the great bulk of the Synoptic Gospels. Each pericope will, in some measure, fall into one of these four categories. And one will notice, on each occasion, that the Triple Tradition material seems to revolve largely around Mark, its 'middle term'; Double Tradition seems to be largely sayings material, often with near-verbatim agreement, and not so similar in its order as Triple Tradition; Special Matthew contains some (so-called) legendary elements and Special Luke is full of great stories, especially parables.

This much is straightforward and it is this that the student should be careful to grasp. When looking at those most simple kinds of material, Special Matthew and Special Luke, however, we saw that difficulties can arise in classifying material. Do certain verses, like Jesus' encounter with John the Baptist in Mt. 3.14-15, fit more obviously in the category 'Special Matthew' or are they, rather, a special Matthaean element embedded in the midst of Triple Tradition?

Further, do pericopae like Luke's Rejection at Nazareth (Lk. 4.16-30), the Call of the First Disciples (Lk. 5.1-11) and the Woman Who Anoints Jesus (Lk. 7.36-50) sit more easily in the L category or should they really to be regarded as distinctive Lukan versions of material that also occurs in Matthew and Mark?

Thus we notice that there is some blurring across the categories. It is usually straightforward to classify a pericope into one type of material or the other, but sometimes the categories are shown not to be watertight. In addition to the issues connected with M and L, the reader should be aware of a further two matters relating to Triple Tradition and Double Tradition.

a. *Not Quite Triple Tradition*

First, there is another kind of material that is not, strictly speaking, Triple Tradition but which is, nevertheless, very closely related to it. We saw above that a great deal of Mark is covered in the general category of Triple Tradition. This means, in other words, that much of Mark is paralleled in both Matthew and Luke. The fact that now needs to be added to this is that some of Mark is paralleled in Matthew but not in Luke and some (but less) of Mark is paralleled in Luke but not in Matthew. Let us take an example of each. This pericope occurs in Matthew and Mark but not in Luke:

Matthew 14.34-36	*Mark 6.53-56*
And when they had crossed over, they came upon the land, to Gennesaret. And when the men of that place recognized him, they sent to the whole of that surrounding region, and they brought to him all those who were ill, and they exhorted him that they might only touch the fringe of his garment. And as many as touched were made well.	And when they had crossed over, they came upon the land of Gennesaret and they moored. And when they got out of the boat, immediately, having recognised him, they ran about the whole of that region, and began to bring those who were ill, wherever they heard that he was. And wherever he came into villages or into cities or into the country, in the market places they laid the sick and exhorted him that even the fringe of his garment they might touch; and as many as touched it were made well.

When coloured this passage has a good deal of purple, in all the places where Matthew and Mark agree.

This pericope occurs in Mark and Luke but not Matthew:

Mark 12.41-44	*Luke 21.1-4*
And having sat down opposite the treasury, he watched how the crowd puts money into the treasury; and many rich people were putting in much. And one poor widow, having approached, put in two copper coins, which is a penny. And having called his disciples to him, he said to them: 'Amen I say to you that this poor widow has put in more than all who have put money into the treasury; for all put in from their abundance, but she from her lack put in all that she has, her whole life'.	And having looked up, he saw the rich putting their gifts into the treasury. And he saw a certain penniless widow, putting there two copper coins, and he said: 'Truly I say to you that this poor widow put in more than all of them; for these all put into the gifts of God from their abundance, but she from her lack has put in all the life that she has'.

When coloured this passage is largely orange—places where Mark and Luke agree.

Material like this, though in two columns and not three, has its closest affinity with Triple Tradition and not, as one might have thought, with Double Tradition. This state of affairs is not as strange as it sounds. Double Tradition, as we saw above, is the technical term used to describe the body of material found in Matthew and Luke *but not in Mark*—so these kind of pericopae, occurring in Matthew and Mark alone, or Mark and Luke alone, are nothing like it. It is much more like Triple Tradition, for Mark is the common element. In colouring terms, both have a 'red' component, Matthew//Mark (blue + red = purple) and Mark//Luke (red + yellow = orange). These passages have no green at all, the characteristic colour of the Double Tradition with its extensive agreement between Matthew and Luke.

This is actually another aspect of Mark's status as the middle term between Matthew and Luke. Nearly all of the material in his Gospel is paralleled in Matthew or Luke or both. The tendency has therefore emerged to think of passages like these (in Matthew and Mark alone, or Mark and Luke alone) as close relatives of pure Triple Tradition passages, especially as the order in these passages remains Mark's order.

In Table 1 above (pp. 35-36), when looking for the first time at the phenomenon of order, we saw a striking pattern across a sample stretch of the Synoptics—an unbroken Markan column in the middle (except for Matthew's M pericope, 17.24-27). This is a key aspect of what it means to say that Mark is the middle term in the Synoptics. Most of the passages in this sample section appear in all three Synoptics—these are pure Triple Tradition—and, what is more, they appear in the same order. Two of the passages (Coming of Elijah; On Offences) occur in Matthew and Mark but not Luke. One (Strange Exorcist) occurs in Mark and Luke but not Matthew, yet all three of these passages, the kind we are considering at present, appear in the Markan sequence. The common thread throughout is Mark.

The same pattern is repeated regularly in the Synoptics. Some scholars have attempted to crystallize the phenomenon into a formula and to say that wherever Matthew departs from Mark's order, Luke keeps to it, and that wherever Luke departs from Mark's order, Matthew keeps to it. There has, however, been a great deal of debate about the use of such formulas. It is difficult to state them neutrally, that is, without assuming one of the solutions to the Synoptic Problem, especially Markan Priority. Further, all too often they tend towards an unhelpful over-simplification of the data. The student may find it more straightforward, therefore, simply to continue to remember the rule that Mark tends to be the middle term among the Synoptics.

Summary

- Some material appears in Matthew and Mark but not Luke; some material appears in Mark and Luke but not Matthew. In colouring terms, these are the passages that feature either lots of purple (Matthew//Mark) or lots of orange (Mark//Luke) and no green at all.
- This material has its closest affinity with the Triple Tradition, because it always appears in Markan order in Matthew and the Markan order in Luke. It is another element of Mark as the middle term.

---

b. *When Mark Is Not the Middle Term*

Unfortunately, however, there are several very important exceptions to the basic rule. On a handful of occasions, Mark is not so clearly the middle term. As always, the best introduction to the data is illustration. The Parable of the Mustard Seed is a classic example of a passage occurring in all three Synoptics in which Mark is not the middle term:

Matthew 13.31-32	Mark 4.30-32	Luke 13.18-19
He put another parable before them, saying: 'The kingdom of heaven is *like a grain of mustard seed, which* **a person, having taken it,** sowed in his field; which, though it is the smallest of all the seeds, when it has grown is the greatest of the vegetables, and it **becomes a tree,** so that *the birds of heaven* come and nest in its **branches'.**	And he was saying, 'How shall we liken the kingdom of God, or in what parable shall we put it? *Like a grain of mustard seed, which* when it is sown upon the earth is the smallest of all the seeds on the earth and when it is sown, it grows and becomes the greatest of all the vegetables, and it produces great branches, so that *the birds of heaven* are able to nest under its shade'.	Therefore he was saying: 'What is the kingdom of God like, and to what shall I liken it? It is *like a grain of mustard seed, which* **a person, having taken it,** put in his own garden and it grew and it **became a tree,** and *the birds of heaven* nested in its **branches'.**

Those who have done their colouring will notice a different pattern here from the pattern observed in the standard Triple Tradition passages discussed above. Where there there were only very little amounts of green, representing the agreement between Matthew and Luke against Mark, here the surprising difference is that there is a great deal more green, representing some substantial agreement between Matthew and Luke against Mark.

The surprise here is that Mark is not the middle term, or, in colouring terms, that there is not a monopoly on brown, purple and orange, the common colours for the passages in which Mark is middle term. There is some clear agreement between all three Synoptics ('like a grain of mustard seed'; 'the birds of heaven', brown), some agreement also between Matthew and Mark alone ('the smallest of all the seeds... the greatest of all the vegetables', purple) and some agreement between Mark and Luke alone ('How shall we liken the kingdom of God, or in what parable shall we put it?', orange), but what is striking is that there is also important agreement between Matthew and Luke against Mark ('which a person, having taken it… becomes/became a tree… branches', green).

Also interesting is the placement of this pericope. Normally, as we saw above, this is the pattern:

MATTHEW	MARK	LUKE
MATTHEW	MARK	
	MARK	LUKE

Mark is usually the common element, which means that one tends not to find agreements in order between Matthew and Luke against Mark. Matters are different here, however, since both Matthew and Luke pair this parable with that of the Leaven (Mt. 13.33//Lk. 13.20-21), a parable that does not appear at all in Mark.

Passages like this, then, Triple Tradition passages in which Mark is not the middle term, appear in all three Synoptics and they feature substantial agreement, either (or sometimes, both) in order and wording, between Matthew and Luke against Mark. Such passages are not very common and isolating them is not always straightforward, not least because the matter of agreement between Matthew and Luke against Mark is simply a question of *degree*. Every Triple Tradition passage features some agreement between Matthew and Luke against Mark. What the interpreter has to decide is whether to call the agreement major (as in the handful of passages currently under discussion) or minor (as in the majority of Triple Tradition passages). These are the passages in which scholars have taken the agreement to be major and not minor, and which therefore constitute examples of Triple Tradition passages in which Mark is not the middle term.

Table 7. *When Mark Is Not the Middle Term*

Matthew	Mark	Luke	Event
3.11-12	1.7-8	3.15-17	John the Baptist
3.13-17	1.9-11	3.21-22	Jesus' Baptism
4.1-11	1.12-13	4.1-13	Temptations
12.22-37	3.22-30	11.14-23	Beelzebub Controversy
13.31-32	4.30-32	13.18-19	Parable of the Mustard Seed
10.1-15	6.6b-13	9.1-6; 10.1-12	Mission of the Disciples

Each of these pericopae features material common to all three Synoptics in addition to some substantial agreement between Matthew and Luke against Mark. In the case of the Temptations and the Mission of the Disciples, the greater bulk of the material is common only to Matthew and Luke.

These passages in which Mark is not the middle term constitute the most difficult phenomenon in the Synoptic Problem. The complexity lies in the fact that this category so blatantly blurs the basic distinction between Triple Tradition and Double Tradition, thus more than anything else preventing the easy classification of everything into the convenient, straightforward categories that would otherwise be possible. Furthermore, scholars are not agreed about the number of these passages, and one's judgement is, as we shall see later, strongly influenced by one's own solution to the Synoptic Problem.

Summary

- There are some Triple Tradition passages in which Mark is not the middle term.
- In other words, there are some passages occurring in all three Synoptics in which there are substantial agreements (not just minor agreements) between Matthew and Luke against Mark in wording and/or order. Such passages, when coloured, have much more green than is usual in Triple Tradition passages.

8. Conclusion

Let us conclude this preliminary exploration by outlining the different kinds of Synoptic material:

(a) *Triple Tradition*: pericopae found in all three Synoptics. The Synopsis is in three columns. The order of this material is similar across the three Synoptics.

(b) *Double Tradition*: pericopae found in Matthew and Luke but not in Mark. The Synopsis has two columns. The order of this material tends to be different in Matthew and Luke.

(c) *Special Matthew*: pericopae found in Matthew alone.

(d) *Special Luke*: pericopae found in Luke alone.[4]

Most of the material in the first three Gospels is easily classified into one of these four types. There are, however, some complications:

(e) *Special Matthew in Triple Tradition contexts*: some material unique to Matthew is embedded in Triple Tradition material and would make no sense outside of that context.

(f) *Special Lukan versions of Triple Tradition*: three pericopae (Rejection at Nazareth; Call of the First Disciples; Anointing) have partial parallels in Matthew and Mark and might be described as special Lukan versions of Triple Tradition material.

(g) *Not quite Triple Tradition*: some pericopae feature in Matthew and Mark but not Luke and some (though fewer) in Mark and Luke but not Matthew. These pericopae are not, strictly speaking, Triple Tradition because they occur in only two Gospels, but they are akin to Triple Tradition because they always appear in the Markan order.

(h) *When Mark is not the Middle Term*: there is some material that is halfway between Triple Tradition and Double Tradition. It appears in all three Synoptics but, unlike pure Triple Tradition, features substantial (rather than minor) agreement between Matthew and Luke.

One of the threads that runs through this is, then, that Mark is often (but not always) *the middle term*. This can be represented like this:

---

4.   It should be added that there is no separate category 'Special Mark'. There is only a handful of verses that occur in Mark alone—chiefly 7.33-36 (Healing of a Deaf Mute); 8.22-26 (Blind Man of Bethsaida); and 14.51-52 (the young man fleeing naked). See further on these pericopae below, pp. 59-61.

MATTHEW	MARK	LUKE
MATTHEW	MARK	
	MARK	LUKE

This phenomenon involves the following:

(a)   In Triple Tradition passages, there are usually substantial agreements in wording between Matthew, Mark and Luke, between Matthew and Mark alone and between Mark and Luke alone. There are only minor agreements between Matthew and Luke against Mark.

(b)   The order of Triple Tradition passages and 'not quite Triple Tradition' passages is usually the same as Mark's order. Matthew and Luke less often agree together in order against Mark.

Some stress, then, needs to be placed on Mark as the middle term if one is to understand the interrelationship of the Gospels. It is a striking phenomenon and it is this issue that provides the most useful starting point in attempting to solve the Synoptic Problem. Now that it is time, then, to turn from describing the data to accounting for it, let us look first at the most common way to account for Mark as the middle term: the theory that his was the first Gospel to be written and that it was used by both Matthew and Luke, the theory known as the Priority of Mark.

Chapter 3

MARKAN PRIORITY

1. *Introduction*

The established canonical order of the Gospels, as many a schoolchild knows, is Matthew, Mark, Luke and John, an order that has been set in stone for a very long time. By happy chance, this order is most conducive to synoptic study, for, as we saw in our previous chapter, Mark is usually the 'middle term' among the Synoptics. Thus, where three columns need to be used, Mark appears in the middle and Matthew and Luke on either side, a situation that often facilitates useful comparison, helping one to see ways in which Mark manifests itself as 'the middle term' among the Synoptics.

Yet this convenient situation masks a more troubling state of affairs, for not only has Matthew long been the first in order among the Gospels, but also his Gospel has been regarded, for most of Christian history, as the earliest Gospel (two matters that are themselves related). This is in stark contrast to more recent history, in which the consensus of scholarly opinion has pronounced strongly in favour of the Priority of Mark. What is it about the internal evidence from the Synoptic Gospels that convinces the majority of scholars that the traditional opinion is wrong? In this chapter we will look carefully at the internal evidence, the Synoptic Gospels themselves, in an attempt to judge the plausibility of the case for Markan Priority. At the end of the chapter we will return briefly to the external evidence.

The procedure will be as follows. Several arguments for Markan Priority will be explained and illustrated and some attempt will be made to point towards the strongest arguments. Before beginning, however, two matters should be noted. First, this chapter does not aim to be exhaustive, but attempts rather to focus on the arguments that are either common, current or in some way compelling. The student looking for a way through the maze should find this approach congenial, for it avoids unnecessary paths that might tempt one away from the key issues. Second, it is important that students know their guide. This book is not a detective novel in which the mystery is solved only at the end of the book, with clues left along the way for the sharp-eyed reader to find. I will not, therefore, hide from the reader where I stand on this, the most important issue in Synoptic studies—strongly on the side of Markan Priority.

2. *Additions and Omissions*

When we are thinking about Markan Priority, there is one question that we need to ask ourselves again and again and it is this: Does the evidence make better sense on the assumption that Mark is writing first, and that his Gospel was used by Matthew and Luke, or does it make better sense on the assumption that he is writing third, and is dependent on Matthew and Luke? These are the two dominant alternatives in Gospel studies, Markan Priority or Markan Posteriority.

One question that naturally arises is whether Mark's Gospel makes better sense on the assumption that its unique elements are matters that Mark has added to Matthew and Luke (Markan Posteriority) or whether its unique elements are matters that Matthew and Luke have each omitted from Mark (Markan Priority). Equally, is the material that is absent from Mark better explained as material that Mark has omitted from Matthew and Luke (Markan Posteriority) or as material that Matthew and Luke have added to Mark (Markan Priority)?

The matter is not an easy one to settle, particularly as one's answers will inevitably be determined by one's perspective on other, prior issues. It often used to be assumed, for example, that the evangelists would have omitted very little of substance from their sources. If they did not include a given pericope or a particular chunk of material, it is because they did not know about it. Mark could not have known about the Birth Narratives (Mt. 1–2; Lk. 1–2) or the Sermon on the Mount (Mt. 5–7) or he would have included them. Indeed this was one of the major presuppositions behind the acceptance of Markan Priority, one that still sometimes makes its presence felt today.

However, in recent years scholars have been more confident about appealing to the creativity of the evangelists, and those with sharp minds can often think of all sorts of reasons that an evangelist may have omitted this or added that. Perhaps, for example, Mark omitted the Sermon on the Mount because it is not consonant with his fast-moving, dramatic narrative, its focus on Jesus as a New Moses hardly congenial to Mark's Jesus, who sits so much more lightly towards the Law. Perhaps he omitted the Birth Narratives because he saw them as similarly surplus to requirements.

Yet a closer, less superficial look at the question of supposed Markan omissions and additions may be more revealing, and may indeed point towards Markan Priority. It will be worth paying special attention, in particular, to the key issue of the relationship between the supposed additions and omissions, asking ourselves whether a coherent picture of Mark the redactor emerges on the assumption that Mark wrote third, using Matthew and Mark as his sources. There are several ways in which Markan Priority explains this data better than does Markan Posteriority. Let us take them in turn.

a. *Apparent Omission of Congenial Material*

If Mark wrote third, using both Matthew and Luke, one will want to know why it is that he omitted so much material from his predecessors. For while there is much material that is common to the three Synoptics (Triple Tradition), there is also a substantial body of material that is in Matthew and Luke alone (Double Tradition). Since the rationale for the writing of Mark has sometimes been stated, by those who think that he wrote third, as being the retaining of concurrent testimony in Matthew and Luke, the question of the omission of Double Tradition material becomes all the more striking. Or, to put it another way, why, on the assumption that Mark wrote third, is there any Double Tradition at all?

Of course the natural answer to this question would be that the Double Tradition pericopae must have been material that was in some way uncongenial to Mark. Our question will therefore be to ask whether the Double Tradition indeed has the character of material that looks uncongenial to the author of Mark's Gospel. Is it defined, on the whole, by 'un-Markan' elements?

It has to be said that the Double Tradition does not obviously have a clearly un-Markan profile. Indeed, there are places in Mark where the insertion of double-tradition might have been highly conducive to his purposes, both literary and theological. Of the several examples that could be given, the clearest is the apparent omission, if one thinks that he knew Matthew and Luke, of the Lord's Prayer. For in Mk 11.20-25, after the fig tree has been withered, there are some Jesus sayings about prayer, including the following:

'So I tell you, whatever you ask for in prayer, believe that you have received it, and it will be yours. Whenever you stand praying, forgive, if you have anything against anyone; so that your Father in heaven may also forgive you your trespasses'.

This might have been an ideal location for Mark to have inserted a version of the Lord's Prayer. The general theme, even some of the specific language is paralleled in Mt. 6.6-13//Lk. 11.2-4. What Mark has done, on the assumption that he knows Matthew, is to take the explanatory words ('if you forgive others...') from Mt. 6.14-15 without taking over the prayer beforehand. In other words, this data does not make good sense on the assumption of Markan Posteriority.

Summary

- Currently the two most popular ways to explain the fact that Mark is usually 'the middle term' are Markan Priority (Matthew's and Luke's use of Mark) or Markan Posteriority (Mark's use of Matthew and Luke). One has to ask whether the evidence makes best sense on the assumption of Markan Priority or Markan Posteriority.
- Some of the material not in Mark makes better sense on the assumption that it has been added by Matthew and/or Luke than on the assumption that it has been omitted by Mark.

b. *Apparent Addition of Elements Not Congenial to Matthew and Luke*
There is little material that is present in Mark but absent in both Matthew and Luke. This is in stark contrast to the substantial amount of material unique to Matthew and the even greater amount of material unique to Luke (see previous chapter). This state of affairs makes the handful of verses that Mark shares with neither of the other Synoptics all the more interesting. The main examples are the following:

Mk 7.33-36: Healing of a Deaf Mute
Mk 8.22-26: Blind Man of Bethsaida
Mk 14.51-52: Man Running Away Naked

The question that we inevitably find ourselves asking is whether it seems more likely that these are passages that have been omitted by Matthew and Luke (Markan Priority) or whether these are passages that have been added by Mark to Matthew and Luke (Markan Posteriority).

It has to be said that Markan Priority seems more likely. The healing of the Deaf Mute features some rather graphic details of Jesus' healing techniques:

> He took him aside in private, away from the crowd, and put his fingers into his ears, and he spat and touched his tongue. Then looking up to heaven he sighed and said to him 'Ephphatha', that is, 'Be opened' (Mk 7.33-34).

Similarly, the Blind Man of Bethsaida is a somewhat bizarre story:

> And they came to Bethsaida. And some people brought to him a blind man, and begged him to touch him. And he took the blind man by the hand, and led him out of the village; and when he had spat on his eyes and laid his hands upon him, he asked him, "Do you see anything?" And he looked up and said, 'I see men; but they look like trees, walking'. Then again he laid his hands upon his eyes; and he looked intently and was restored, and saw everything clearly. And he sent him away to his home, saying, 'Do not even enter the village' (Mk 8.22-26).

As in the healing of the Deaf Mute, Jesus' healing technique involves the use of saliva. Mark's Jesus here contrasts somewhat with both Matthew's and Luke's Jesus. Nowhere in Matthew or Luke do we find healings of this type, using physical agents like saliva. It may well be that they both had distaste for this kind of depiction of Jesus. But we have other features too that are more straightforwardly explained on Markan Priority than they are on Markan Posteriority. Notice the element of secrecy involved in both healings. 'Do not even enter the village', Jesus tells the healed blind man, just as he had told the healed deaf-mute 'to tell no-one' (Mk 8.36). These elements of secrecy are much more scarce in Matthew and Luke than they are in Mark.

Furthermore, this story might seem to place some kind of limit on Jesus' ability—the healing is not instantaneous but takes time. This is not the only time that Jesus' power appears to be limited in Mark's Gospel. Similarly, in 6.5, after the incident at the synagogue in his home country, we read 'And he *could do no* mighty work there, except that he laid his hands upon a few sick people and healed them', a passage that reads differently in Mt. 13.58 where Jesus '*did not do* many deeds of power there, because of their unbelief'. The Markan Jesus is a more human Jesus, a more earthly and realistic Jesus, and it is reasonable to imagine Matthew (and Luke) amending and omitting what was before them. And Christian history has, on the whole, been much more strongly influenced by their picture of Jesus than by Mark's.

Could Mark have added this material to Matthew and Luke? Of course he could. Perhaps he was eager to correct the more reverential picture of Matthew and Luke, thus in a sense 'reprimitivizing' the tradition. The question, however, is whether this view, on which Mark adds only a small number of archaizing traditions at the expense of much congenial material in Matthew and Luke, is more plausible than the alternative possibility, that these incidents are ones omitted by Matthew and Luke in accordance with their general redactional policies. Most would feel that Markan Priority makes better sense of the data than does Markan Posteriority.

It might added that in this category, as in several of the others, we consistently run into difficulties over the question of Mark's profile. For if Mark's purpose is to include in his Gospel those stories to which his predecessors bear concurrent testimony, then we find ourselves asking what it is about these stories, the Blind Man of Bethsaida and the Deaf Mute, that is so important that they beg to be added. If, on the other hand, Mark is eager to add material that he considers of interest, without concern over the united testimony of his predecessors, why does so little else make it into the Gospel? Is it that Mark did not know of any other useful stories?

Summary

- The material unique to Mark makes better sense as material omitted by Matthew and Luke than it does as material added by Mark.

c. *The Place of Oral Tradition*

This problem is illustrated and so compounded further by questions over the place of oral tradition in Christian origins. On the assumption that Matthew is writing first, there appears to be a wealth of material available to him. Similarly for Luke, on the assumption that he has used only Matthew, there appears to be a large amount of additional tradition available. Then, however, when Mark writes, as we have seen, there seems to be a striking lack of additional material available to the author. All he adds is a small handful of stories, none of which is particularly striking. And he adds virtually no fresh sayings material at all. Those who believe that Mark came third therefore have to make sense of a situation in which Mark stands out from much of early Christianity. For after Mark, in the early second century, Papias reports that he prefers what he calls 'the living voice' to the written word.[1] And the recent discovery (in 1945) of the Gospel of Thomas,[2] which features a good deal of material independent of the Synoptics and apparently gleaned from oral tradition would seem to confirm further that oral tradition did not die a death somewhere in the late first century. Why does Mark apparently rely on this oral tradition so little? Were the stories of the Blind Man of Bethsaida and the Deaf Mute the best he could manage?

This troubling situation is intensified by a striking feature of Mark's style. For of all the (canonical) Gospels, Mark's is the most blatantly colloquial, the most 'oral' in nature. His Gospel often sounds like it is directly dependent on oral traditions, with its lively pace (*and immediately...*), its present tenses (*and Jesus says...*), its love of visual detail ('the green grass', Mk 6.39; 'he was in the stern, asleep on the cushion', 4.38) and its abrupt ending (16.8). It is perhaps for these reasons, as well as for reasons of length, that Mark has been the Gospel that has lent itself most readily in modern times to oral performance. In other words, it would be odd if the most 'oral' of the Synoptic Gospels turned out also to be the third Gospel, dependent almost entirely (save for a handful of verses) on two much more literary predecessors, both of whom, like those who also came later, apparently had rich access to oral traditions of Jesus' actions and sayings.

Summary

- If Mark has only added the material that is unique to him, then his Gospel becomes an anomaly in early Christianity, with relatively little contact with oral tradition in comparison with Matthew, Luke, Thomas and others.

1.   Papias is quoted by the fourth century Church historian Eusebius, *Ecclesiastical History* 3.39.1-7, 14-17.

2.   Greek fragments of the Gospel of Thomas probably dating to the early third century were found at Oxyrhynchus, Egypt, in 1897. A complete copy of the same Gospel in Coptic, dating from the fourth century, was found at Nag Hammadi, Egypt, in 1945. The Gospel is a collection of Jesus' sayings and it originated somewhere between the late first and mid second century.

d. *The Relationship between Omissions and Additions*

The question of Mark's alleged omissions and additions can be most clearly focused by asking about the relationship between them. Does a consistent or coherent picture of Mark the redactor emerge when we consider his Gospel from the perspective of the Griesbach Theory, in which Mark utilizes Matthew and Luke?

As we have seen, Mark, on this theory, apparently adds material that would have been in any case uncongenial to Matthew and Luke (Blind Man of Bethsaida, etc.), material that seems an odd selection from what, one presumes, would have been available to him from his oral tradition. These few additions are balanced by the omission of congenial material like the Lord's Prayer, for which Mark has an obvious context into which it might have been slotted. The picture that is emerging does not seem to favour the posteriority of Mark. But this negative judgment is compounded still further by noticing that on the Griesbach Theory, Mark's tendencies pull very much in opposite directions.

If Mark is the third evangelist to write and not the first, then we need to find a way of making sense of two features of his Gospel. First, he has a tendency, on occasions, to add clarificatory material to his sources in Matthew and Luke, as here for example:

Matthew 9.10	*Mark 2.15*	*Luke 5.29*
And as he sat at table in the house, behold, many tax collectors and sinners came and sat down with Jesus and his disciples.	And as he sat at table in his house, many tax collectors and sinners were sitting with Jesus and his disciples; *for there were many who followed him.*	And Levi made him a great feast in his house; and there was a large company of tax collectors and others sitting at table with them.

Mark often adds little explanatory clauses like this. At 11.13, for example, the narrator says, 'When he came to it, he found nothing but leaves, *for it was not the season for figs*'. At 16.4 we hear, 'And looking up, they saw that the stone was rolled back, *for it was very large*'. And right at the beginning of the Gospel Mark explains that Jesus 'saw Simon and his brother Andrew casting a net into the sea *for they were fishermen*' (1.16).[3]

3.　　The '*for...*' clauses do not occur in Matthew's parallels to Mk 11.13 (in

The adding of these somewhat redundant clarificatory clauses would appear to bear witness to an evangelist who is eager to spell out things very carefully for the reader. This looks like someone who, on the assumption of the Griesbach Theory, is editing Matthew and Luke to draw out what often appears to be transparently obvious. It is striking, therefore, that elsewhere Mark—again on the assumption of his use of Matthew and Luke—appears to be doing precisely the opposite thing, and making his sources more enigmatic, more darkly ironic, especially in the Passion Narrative.

One thinks, for example, of the following passage, in which there is a subtlety about Mark's account that is lacking in Matthew and Luke:

Matthew 26.67-68	Mark 14.65	Luke 22.64
Then they spat into his face, and struck him; and some slapped him, saying, 'Prophesy to us, you Christ! *Who is it that struck you?*'	And some began to spit on him, and to cover his face, and to strike him, saying to him, 'Prophesy!' And the guards received him with blows.	Now the men who were holding Jesus mocked him and beat him; they also blindfolded him and asked him, 'Prophesy! *Who is it that struck you?*

Mark's account here has a wonderful, dark dramatic irony, an irony that we can only perceive when we view this passage in context. People are spitting on Jesus, striking him and saying 'Prophesy!', little realizing that they are in the act of fulfilling Jesus' own prophecy of 10.34, 'they will mock him, and spit upon him, and flog him, and kill him'. Likewise, as this action is going on, Peter is in the act of fulfilling the prophecy of 14.30 ('this day, this very night, before the cock crows twice you will deny me three times').

In Matthew and Luke there is none of this irony, and the mocking charge to 'Prophesy!' is explicated by means of a clarificatory question, 'Who is it who smote you?' (Mt. 26.68; Lk. 22.64), the 'prophesying' relating now purely to the issue of second sight. This makes good sense on the assumption of Markan Priority but less sense on the Griesbach Theory, for which Mark avoids the concurrent testimony of Matthew and Luke and subtly creates a more darkly ironic scene. The latter is of

Mt. 21.19) and Mk 16.4 (in Mt. 28.4), but it is present in Matthew's parallel to Mk 1.16 (in Mt. 4.18).

course possible, but it is at variance with the view of Mark that we pick up elsewhere from his addition of somewhat banal clarificatory elements. There is an interesting, apparently inconsistent combination of subtlety in omission and editing with the more banal and redundant kind of clarificatory addition.

The difficulty, in short, for the Griesbach Theory in dealing with Mark's alleged omissions and additions is that so many contrasting features of Mark are placed into such very sharp relief. Mark is a fascinating Gospel, in some ways mysterious, in other ways banal, often prosaic, frequently profound. Is it more likely that this is a work of brutish genius, the first attempt to write a 'gospel of Jesus Christ' (1.1) by imposing a narrative on disparate traditional materials, or is this the complex product of contradictory elements in a redactional procedure, utilizing Matthew and Luke, that is rarely easy to fathom? Often, on the theory that Mark wrote third, there seems to be a deliberate rejection of the concurrent testimony of Matthew and Luke that on the Griesbach Theory he is supposed to value, in order simply to add almost redundant clarificatory clauses, something that appears to be contradicted by his very careful and subtle work elsewhere. In this category, Markan Priority is the preferable option.

Summary

- If one assumes Markan Posteriority, the relationship between the supposed omissions and additions does not make for a coherent picture of Markan redaction. The addition of banal clarificatory additions is not consonant with the generally enigmatic, ironic tone of Mark's Gospel. It is more likely that Mark was the first Gospel to be written, a work of brutish genius, which was subsequently explicated by both Matthew and Luke.

3. *Harder Readings*

If the evidence from supposed additions and omissions therefore tends to point in the direction of Markan Priority, is this tendency supported in other ways? When Mark parallels material in Matthew and/or Luke, for example, who among the three has what one might call the 'harder' reading? This will be a case, once more, of the individual reader's judgment, and of asking whether Mark looks more like the document from which Matthew and Luke worked, or more like a document based on Matthew and Luke.

In this category, most scholars have concluded that Mark often has the more difficult reading, the kind of text that was more difficult for later Christians to accept, and so more likely to have been corrected by others than to have been a correction of others. As always, it is easier to see the point when it is illustrated. Let us look then at a handful of examples of Triple Tradition (or 'not quite Triple Tradition' passages) that make the point clearly.

Matthew 8.16-17	*Mark 1.32-34*	*Luke 4.40-41*
That evening	That evening, at sundown,	Now when the sun was setting,
they brought to him many who were possessed with demons;	they brought to him all who were sick or possessed with demons. And the whole city was	all those who had any that were sick with various diseases brought them to him;
and he cast out the spirits with a word, and healed all who were sick. This was to fulfil what was spoken by the prophet Isaiah, 'He took our infirmities and bore our diseases'.	gathered together about the door. And he healed many who were sick with various diseases, and cast out many demons;	and he laid his hands on every one of them and healed them. And demons also came out of many, crying, 'You are the Son of God!' But he rebuked them, and would not allow them to speak,
	and he would not permit the demons to speak, because they knew him.	because they knew that he was the Christ.

There are several features of interest in this pericope (which also has parallels in Mt. 12.15-16, Mk 3.10-12 and Lk. 6.17-19 and elsewhere), one of which is the distinction between the number of people healed in the different accounts. In both Matthew ('all') and Luke ('each one'), everyone is healed, whereas in Mark it is 'many' who are healed. What one has to ask under such circumstances is, once more, what is more likely? Has Mark, writing third, changed the clear indication that Jesus healed everybody who came to him to the more ambiguous line that Jesus healed 'many'? Or are we to think that Matthew and Luke have both clarified their source by making clear all were healed and that there was no one who missed out? Most will think that Markan Priority provides the more likely scenario here.

The following example is in some ways similar. Although the general pericope is paralleled in Luke (Mt. 13.54-58//Mk 6.1-6a//Lk. 4.16-30), his Gospel has no specific parallel to this verse. This example therefore comes in two columns:

Matthew 13.58	Mark 6.5
And he did not do many mighty works there,	And he could do no mighty work there, except that he laid his hands upon a few sick people and healed them. And he
because of their unbelief.	marvelled because of their unbelief.

As often, Matthew's differences from Mark here are slight but significant. Whereas in Mark the clear impression is that Jesus is unable to do mighty works there, in Matthew we hear rather that Jesus simply 'did not' do any mighty works. It is a small but striking point that is usually held to point towards Markan Priority. It is straightforward to imagine Matthew making the change here, but stranger to think of Mark making the change in the opposite direction.

In a way this category is an extension of the previous category, for the reader is being called upon to ask about direction of dependence. Is it more plausible that Mark is creating his text on the basis of Matthew and Luke? Or is it more plausible that Matthew and Luke are creating their texts on the basis of Mark? Most think it more likely that Matthew and Luke have omitted a handful of strange Markan pericopae than that Mark added the odd pericopae to his united witness in Matthew and Luke. So also here most think it more likely that Matthew and Luke have rewritten the 'harder' Markan material than that the reverse happened. As in the previous category, therefore, this evidence is suggestive rather than decisive, plausible if not provable.

Summary

- In several difficult passages, it is more straightforward to see Mark as the source for Matthew and Luke than it is to see Matthew and Luke as the sources for Mark.

4. *The Dates of the Gospels*

It is a notorious difficulty in Synoptic Studies to work out precisely when the Gospels were written. It is clear that they were all in existence by the early to mid second century, when we begin to hear quotations from them, but we would like to be able to pinpoint the date more accurately. If it were clear, for example, that the best evidence placed Mark's Gospel earlier than Matthew's or Luke's, we would have a useful additional reason for thinking that his Gospel was the first to be written.

Although the evidence is inconclusive, the few hints that we have are that Mark's Gospel is earlier than Matthew's and Luke's. The most decisive pointer is the question of whether or not the Gospels refer, however obliquely, to the key events of 70 CE, when Jerusalem was overrun by the Roman army after the Jewish War beginning in 66 CE. Matthew and Luke both seem to provide hints that they know of the events of 70. These are the clearest examples:

Matthew 23.37-39	*Luke 13.34-35*
'Jerusalem, Jerusalem, killing the prophets and stoning those who are sent to you! How often would I have gathered your children together as a hen gathers her brood under her wings, and you would not! Behold, your house is forsaken and desolate. For I tell you, you will not see me again, until you say, "Blessed is he who comes in the name of the Lord!"'	'Jerusalem, Jerusalem, killing the prophets and stoning those who are sent to you! How often would I have gathered your children together as a hen gathers her brood under her wings, and you would not! Behold, your house is forsaken. And I tell you, you will not see me until you say, "Blessed is he who comes in the name of the Lord!"'

Here Matthew and Luke, in a Double Tradition passage (note the close verbal agreement), seem to have Jesus prophetically announcing dramatic events to take place in Jerusalem, and these are words that would have much more poignancy in a post-70 situation. 'Your house', Jerusalem's house, clearly refers to the Temple, which in the post-70 period indeed lay 'forsaken' and in ruins. That does not necessarily mean that Matthew and Luke, or their tradition, were putting words into Jesus' mouth, but it may mean that both evangelists have taken care to include material that will have a special poignancy for their hearers.

But is there anything more specific than this? Well, the Parable of the Great Banquet in Matthew's Gospel (which has a parallel also in Lk. 14.15-24 and Thomas 64) features an interesting verse that may allude to the events of 70 CE:

> Again he sent other servants, saying, 'Tell those who are invited, 'Behold, I have made ready my dinner, my oxen and my fat calves are killed, and everything is ready; come to the marriage feast'.' But they made light of it and went off, one to his farm, another to his business, while the rest seized his servants, treated them shamefully, and killed them. *The king was angry, and he sent his troops and destroyed those murderers and burned their city.* Then he said to his servants, 'The wedding is ready, but those invited were not worthy' (Mt. 22.4-8).

The thing that is so striking here is the extent to which this element intrudes into a story that can be told quite adequately without it (as in Luke and Thomas). It may be that Matthew is thinking here of the fall of Jerusalem.

Such elements appear to be lacking, on the other hand, in Mark. Indeed, where Mark is in parallel to Matthew and Luke, it appears likely that Matthew and Luke have redacted Mark in the light of the events of 70:

Matthew 24.15; 21-22	Mark 13.14; 19-20	Luke 21.20-21; 23-24
'So when you see the desolating sacrilege spoken of by the prophet Daniel, standing in the holy place (let the reader understand), then let those who are in Judea flee to the mountains…	'But when you see the desolating sacrilege set up where it ought not to be (let the reader understand), then let those who are in Judea flee to the mountains…	'But when you see Jerusalem surrounded by armies, then know that its desolation has come near. Then let those who are in Judea flee to the mountains…
For then there will be great tribulation, such as has not been from the beginning of the world until now, no, and never will be. And if those days had not been shortened, no human	For in those days there will be such tribulation as has not been from the beginning of the creation which God created until now, and never will be. And if the Lord had not shortened the days, no human	For great distress shall be upon the earth and wrath upon this people; they will fall by the edge of the sword, and be led captive among all nations; and Jerusalem

being would be saved; but	being would be saved; but	will be trodden down by
for the sake of the elect	for the sake of the elect,	the Gentiles, until the
those days will be	whom he chose, he	times of the Gentiles are
shortened.'	shortened the days.'	fulfilled.'

It is clear that Luke in particular is more specific than Mark. Whereas Mark's Jesus speaks obliquely about the 'desolating sacrilege set up where it ought not to be', Luke's Jesus prophesies a Jerusalem surrounded by armies and downtrodden by 'the Gentiles'. It would seem that of all the evangelists, Mark is the least explicit about the events of 70. This is, of course, only a potential indicator of Markan Priority. It is not decisive. The point is that, as usual, in so far as there is any indicator present, it goes in the direction of Markan Priority over Matthew and Luke.

Are there then any other internal indications of Mark's age that might help us? One hint is the note, which does not appear in either Matthew or Luke, that Simon of Cyrene, who carried Jesus' cross, was 'the father of Alexander and Rufus' (Mk 15.21):

Matthew 27.32	*Mark 15.21*	*Luke 23.26*
And after coming out, they found a man from Cyrene, named Simon;	And they are compelling a certain passer-by, Simon of Cyrene coming from the country, *the father of Alexander and Rufus*,	And as they led him away, seizing a certain Simon of Cyrene coming from the country,
they compelled this man in order that he might carry his cross.	in order that he might carry his cross.	they laid the cross on him to carry behind Jesus.

This passing reference to 'Alexander and Rufus' is interesting in that it is not standard practice to mention a given individual's children. Usually characters are identified by the name of their father (James and John as 'sons of Zebedee', for example). The only obvious reason for mentioning a character's children is that the children are expected to be known by the reader. Here, then, we have a hint that Mark's Gospel does not perceive itself to be a long way, in time, from the events it is relating, for the sons of one of the characters in the story are apparently known to Mark's readers. There are no such indications in Matthew or Luke. Of course this may not count for a great deal, but once more it is the case that, in so far as there are any indicators at all, they go in the favour of Markan Priority.

Summary

- In so far as there are any internal indications of the dates of composition of the Gospels, they suggest that Matthew and Luke are later than Mark.

---

5. *Circumstantial Evidence*

So far we have seen that a variety of indicators seem to point towards Markan Priority. When looking at patterns of omission and addition, it seems more likely that Matthew and Luke postdate Mark than that Mark postdates Matthew and Luke. Mark also tends to include the 'harder' readings when we compare it with Matthew and Luke and, further, where there is evidence of the dates of the Gospels, what we have points in the direction of Markan Priority. However, there is a troubling feature in all of this discussion. All of these features are merely suggestive. Not one of them appears decisive.

The difficulty is this. Most scholars feel that because Markan Priority explains so much of the data so well, it is without doubt the 'chief suspect' in the case. Yet when it comes to looking for clear and decisive indicators, all that scholars, on the whole, have been able to find is circumstantial evidence. What we would like is something that does not merely point the finger, but actually secures the conviction. We need something decisive. We need fingerprints on the gun. Happily, there is one fresh category left to consider, that of editorial fatigue in Matthew and Luke. Previous scholars had seen hints of this but until recently its potential for solving the Synoptic Problem had not been realized.

6. *Securing a Conviction: Editorial Fatigue*

When one writer is copying the work of another, changes are sometimes made at the beginning of an account that are not sustained throughout. The writer lapses into docile reproduction of the source. Like continuity errors in film and television, editorial fatigue results in unconscious mistakes, small errors of detail that naturally arise in the course of constructing a narrative. This phenomenon of 'fatigue' is thus a telltale sign of a writer's dependence on a source. The best way to explain the phenomenon is to illustrate it. Let us therefore return to one of our examples from Triple Tradition material, the story of the Leper:

Matthew 8.1-4	Mark 1.40-45	Luke 5.12-16
1. When he came down from the mountain, *many crowds followed him;*		And it came to pass while he was in one of the cities
2. and behold, a leper	40. And a leper	and behold, a man full of leprosy; and having seen Jesus,
came to him and	came to him, beseeching him and bending his knee, saying,	he fell before his face saying,
knelt before him, saying, 'Lord, if you will, you can make me clean'.	to him, 'If you will, you are able to cleanse me'.	'Lord, if you will, you are able to cleanse me'.
3. And he stretched out his hand and touched him, saying, 'I will; be clean'.	41. Moved with anger, he stretched out his hand and touched him, and said to him, 'I will; be clean'.	13. And he stretched out his hand, and touched him, saying, 'I will; be clean'.
And immediately his leprosy was cleansed. 4. And Jesus said to him,	42. And immediately the leprosy left him, and he was made clean. 43. And he sternly charged him, and sent him away at once, 44. and said to him,	And immediately the leprosy left him. 14. And he charged him
<u>'See that you say nothing to any one</u>; but go, show yourself to the priest, and offer the gift	<u>'See that you say nothing to any one</u>; but go, show yourself to the priest, and offer for your cleansing	to tell no one; but 'go and show yourself to the priest, and make an offering for your cleansing,
that Moses commanded, for a proof to the people'.	what Moses commanded, for a proof to the people'.	as Moses commanded, for a proof to the people'.

In Matthew's version of the story there are two elements that are difficult to reconcile: *many crowds* at the beginning of the narrative (8.1) and the charge 'See that you say nothing to any one' at the end of it (8.4). A miracle that has been witnessed by many is apparently to be kept secret. This is in contrast to Mark where there are no crowds. The Markan leper meets Jesus privately and the command to silence is coherent.

This odd state of affairs can be explained by the theory of Markan

Priority, for which this is therefore evidence. This is what seems to have happened. Matthew has just featured three chapters of largely non-Markan teaching material (Mt. 5–7, the Sermon on the Mount) and here he is returning to Triple Tradition (Markan) material. He resets the scene by making a characteristic Matthean change, introducing 'many crowds' (Mt. 8.1; cf. 4.25; 13.2; 15.30; 19.2; never found in Mark). But as he goes on telling the story, docile reproduction of his source, or editorial fatigue, causes him to reproduce a feature not consonant with his new introduction to it. This example is particularly striking in that the 'secrecy theme' ('See that you say nothing to any one') is such a vivid and major theme in Mark's Gospel (e.g. 1.34; 3.12; 5.43; 7.36; 8.30), but is much less common in Matthew. It seems likely that Matthew has made characteristic changes to Mark at the beginning of the pericope, changes that lead the account into inconsistency when Matthew reproduces the characteristically Markan wording at the end of the pericope.

And this is not an isolated example. One that seems similarly persuasive is the story of the Death of John the Baptist (Mk 6.14-29//Mt. 14.1-12). For Mark, Herod is always 'king', four times in the passage (Mk 6.22, 25, 26, 27). Matthew apparently corrects this to 'tetrarch' (Mt. 14.1). This is a good move: Herod Antipas was not a king but a petty dependent prince and he is called 'tetrarch' by the Jewish historian Josephus (*Ant.* 17.188; 18. 102, 109, 122). This kind of precision is typical of Matthew. Later, he will specify that Pilate (Mk 15.1, 4, 9, 12, 14, 15, 43, 44) is properly called 'the governor' (Mt. 27.2, 11, 14, 15, 21, 27, 28.14), and 'the high priest' (Mk 14.53) is 'Caiaphas the high priest' (Mt. 26.57). Earlier, in his Birth Narrative, Matthew tells us that Herod the Great is a 'king' (2.1, 3) and that Archelaus is not (2.22). More is the shame, then, that Matthew lapses into calling Herod 'the king' halfway through the story of John the Baptist's death (Mt. 14.9), in agreement with Mark (6.26).

There is, further, a more serious inconsistency in the same verse. The story in Mark is that Herodias wanted to kill John because she had a grudge against him: 'But she could not because Herod feared John, knowing that he was a righteous and holy man, and he protected him. When he heard him, he was greatly perplexed; and yet he liked to listen to him'. (Mk 6.19-20). In Matthew's version of the story, this element has dropped out: now it is Herod and not Herodias who wants him killed (Mt. 14.5). When Mark, then, speaks of Herod's 'grief' at the request for John's head, it is coherent and understandable: Herodias demanded something that Herod did not want. But when Matthew in parallel speaks of the king's grief (Mt. 14.9), it makes no sense at all. Matthew had told us, after all, that 'Herod wanted to put him to death' (14.5).

The obvious explanation for the inconsistencies of Matthew's account is that he is working from a source. He has made changes in the early stages that he fails to sustain throughout, thus betraying his knowledge of Mark. This is particularly plausible when one notes that Matthew's account is considerably shorter than Mark's: Matthew has overlooked important details in the act of abbreviating.

But to be sure about Markan Priority, we will need examples of the same thing from Luke's alleged use of Mark. We will not be disappointed. First, the Parable of the Sower and its Interpretation (Mt. 13.1-23//Mk 4.1-20//Lk. 8.4-15) present exactly the kind of scenario where, on the theory of Markan Priority, one would expect to see some incongruities. The evangelists would need to be careful to sustain any changes made in their retelling of the parable into the interpretation that follows.

On three occasions, Luke apparently omits features of Mark's Parable that he goes on to mention in the Interpretation. First, Mark says that the seed that fell on rocky soil sprang up quickly because it had no depth of earth (Mk 4.5; cf. Lk. 8.6). Luke omits to mention this, yet he has the corresponding section in the Interpretation, 'those who when they hear, with joy they receive the word' (Lk. 8.13; cf. Mk 4.16).

Second, in Lk. 8.6, the seed 'withered for lack of moisture'. This is a different reason from the one in Mark where it withers 'because it had no root' (Mk 4.6). In the Interpretation, however, Luke apparently reverts to the Markan reason:

Mark 4.17	*Luke 8.13*
'And they have no root in themselves but last only for a little while'.	'And these have no root; they believe for a while'.

Third, the sun is the agent of the scorching in Mark (4.6). This is then interpreted as 'trouble or persecution'. Luke does not have the sun (8.6) but he does have 'temptation' that interprets it (Lk. 8.13).

In short, these three features of the Parable of the Sower show clearly that Luke has an interpretation to a text that interprets features that are not in that text. He has made changes in the Parable, changes that he has not been able to sustain in the Interpretation. This is a good example of the phenomenon of fatigue, which only makes sense on the theory of Markan Priority.

For a second example of Lukan fatigue, let us look at the Healing of the Paralytic (Mt. 9.1-8//Mk 2.1-12//Lk. 5.17-26). Here, Luke's introduction to the story of the Paralytic (Mk 2.1-12//Lk. 5.17-26) is quite characteristic. 'And it came to pass on one of those days, and he was teaching' (Lk. 5.17) is the kind of general, vague introduction to a pericope common in Luke who often gives the impression that a given incident is one among that could have been related. But in rewriting this introduction, Luke omits to mention entry into a house, unlike Mark in 2.1, which has the subsequent comment, 'Many were gathered together, so that there was no longer room for them, not even about the door' (Mk 2.2). In agreement with Mark, however, Luke has plot developments that require Jesus to be in a crowded house of exactly the kind Mark mentions:

Mark 2.4	Luke 5.19
'And when they could not get near him because of the crowd, they removed the roof above him; and when they had made an opening, they let down the pallet on which the paralytic lay'.	'Finding no way to bring him in, because of the crowd, they went up on the roof and let him down with his bed through the tiles into the midst before Jesus'.

Continuity errors like this are natural when a writer is dependent on the work of another. Luke omits to mention Mark's house and his inadvertence results in men ascending the roof of a house that Jesus has not entered.

It might be added, as further evidence from the same pericope, that Luke has the scribes and the Pharisees debating not, as in Mark, 'in their hearts' (Mk 2.6) but, apparently, aloud (Lk. 5.21). This is in spite of the fact that Jesus goes on to question them, in both Luke and Mark, why they have been debating 'in' their 'hearts' (Mk 2.8//Lk. 5.22). The latter phrase seems simply to have come in, by fatigue, from Mark.

This evidence of editorial fatigue provides, then, some strong evidence for Markan Priority. Matthew and Luke apparently rewrite in characteristic ways the beginning of pericopae taken over from Mark, only to lapse into the wording of the original as they proceed, creating minor inconsistencies and betraying the identity of their source. It is just the kind of evidence one might wish for—a clear, decisive indicator of Markan Priority that will not make good sense on the assumption that Mark wrote third. It seems that we have the fingerprints on the gun.

Summary

- The most decisive indicator of Markan Priority is evidence of editorial fatigue in Matthew and Luke. It seems that as Matthew and Luke rewrote passages from Mark, they made characteristic changes in the early part of pericopae, lapsing into Mark's wording later in the same pericopae, so producing an inconsistency or an incoherence that betrayed their knowledge of Mark.

7. The Patristic Evidence

However, as I mentioned at the beginning of this chapter, there is something rather troubling about the case for Markan Priority, a niggling difficulty that contradicts the scholarly consensus: the external evidence. All the early Christian writers who expressed an opinion, from the late second century onwards, pronounced in favour of the priority of Matthew. Perhaps most importantly, Irenaeus, the bishop of Lyons, who was writing towards the end of the second century, clearly dates Matthew before Mark. In the earliest surviving statement concerning the order in which the Gospels were composed, he says that 'Matthew' was written among Hebrews and in their language 'while Peter and Paul were preaching and founding the church in Rome', whereas Mark wrote 'after their departure' (or 'decease', Greek: *exodos*).[4] Likewise, Clement, Origen, Augustine and Jerome, writing in the third to the fifth centuries, all witness to Matthaean Priority. There is a genuine consensus here, a consensus far stronger than the current scholarly one concerning the Priority of Mark. Given this unanimity, and given the relatively early nature of this evidence, would it not be foolish to ignore it?

Adherents of the Griesbach Theory have stressed this unanimity in the Patristic evidence and it is undoubtedly one of the strongest elements in favour of their theory. It is not enough, however, to overturn

4.   *Against Heresies* 3.11.7; quoted in Eusebius, *Ecclesiastical History* 5.8.

the weight of the internal evidence, for several reasons. First, we need to notice that in this kind of context, the internal evidence has to be key. Of course we should not ignore the external evidence, but in critical scholarship we should not be afraid of cross-examining it or of looking to see whether it is corroborated by the internal evidence. The point is best made by means of an analogy. If present-day students do what the evangelists did in the first century, copying large stretches of the work of others without acknowledging their sources, we call it plagiarism, and it is regarded as a serious offence in higher education because one wants to be sure that it is indeed a student's work and not somebody else's when one is assessing it. Now if one student were to accuse another of plagiarism, we would listen to the charge but we would not institute disciplinary proceedings unless we were quite sure of the plagiarism on the internal evidence generated by the student's piece of work itself. In other words, we would take the (external) evidence of the accusation seriously, but we would not think of penalizing the student concerned unless we were able to find clear evidence of plagiarism in the piece of work itself. It is the same with the Synoptic Gospels. We listen to the external evidence, but if it does not square with the overwhelming internal evidence, we have no choice but to place a question mark against it.

Leaving the situation like this, though, is not adequate. There are still unanswered questions. The good historian needs to ask how the sources came to say what they say. Why do these sources pronounce in favour of the priority of Matthew? Did they know what had happened? It is usually assumed that these fathers did not have a special knowledge of the order of the composition of the Gospels. Originally, someone made some inferences from the knowledge they did have, and these inferences soon became the basis for a steady, repeated tradition, itself confirmed by the Fathers making similar inferences from the same material.

The major concern in this early period was not so much the one that concerns us when we are looking at the Synoptic Problem, the question of *when* the Gospels were written and how they were related to one another. Their major concern was the question of *who* wrote the Gospels, without any pressing interest in how they related to one another. Given a plethora of other gospels, the fathers wanted to establish grounds for maintaining the authority of these four, and the key issue became the one of apostolic authorship or connection. The fathers wanted to demonstrate that the four Gospels they favoured were written by the apostles, or, at the very least, under the influence of the apostles. The relative dates given to the Gospels then arose largely as a consequence of prior decisions on the identity of the authors. From the second century onwards, Matthew was not only the most popular Gospel but it was also the one that bore the name of an apostle. Mark and Luke, on the other hand, did not bear the names of apostles and were thought to have been written by the companions of Peter and Paul respectively. The Priority of Matthew was a natural consequence of the belief that his Gospel was the one directly written by an apostle. Likewise, the idea that Mark and Luke both postdated Matthew was the natural consequence of the belief that their Gospels were in a way secondary, written not by but under the influence of the apostles.[5]

Scholars now doubt quite strongly that the Gospels were written by or even under the direct influence of the apostles. It is likely that the Gospels were originally anonymous and that the ascriptions 'According to Matthew', 'According to Mark', 'According to Luke' and 'According to John' were only added later, and perhaps based only on inferences derived from the New Testament texts themselves.[6] Only Matthew tells the story of the Call of Matthew (9.9-10; the same character is called 'Levi' in Mark and Luke) and the ascription to that apostle may have been inferred from this. Similarly, Mark's link to Peter may have been the result of an inference based on 1 Pet. 5.13, in which Peter refers to 'my son Mark'; and Luke is linked to Paul because of the 'we' passages in the second half of Acts combined with references to a Luke in Colossians and Philemon.

But however the fathers came to decide on these names (and there is no tradition of any variation), there is an interesting distinction between Matthew on the one hand and Mark and Luke on the other. The one Gospel bears the name of an apostle where the other two do not. Could it be that priority was accorded to the Gospel that was apostolic? If so, we might expect to see some disagreement over the relative priority of Mark and Luke. And this indeed is what we do see. For while Irenaeus (above) does not pronounce on the relative order of

---

5.   Although John's Gospel, which also bears the name of an apostle, was usually thought of as the last of the four, there was also a strong tradition that the apostle John lived to an old age, and that the Fourth Gospel was relatively late.

6.   Note, however, Martin Hengel's spirited defence of the notion that the ascriptions *kata Matthaion* (according to Matthew) etc. are early and reliable (*Studies in the Gospel of Mark* [ET; London: SCM Press, 1985], pp. 64-84).

Mark and Luke, later writers did do so. Origen, writing in the middle of the third century, seems to place Mark before Luke:

> The first written [gospel] was that according to Matthew, who was once a toll-collector but later an apostle of Jesus Christ. He published it for those who became believers from Judaism, since it was composed in the Hebrew language. The second was that according to Mark, who wrote it according to Peter's instructions. Peter also acknowledged him as his son in his general letter, saying in these words: 'She who is in Babylon, chosen with you, sends you greetings; and so does my son Mark' [1 Pet. 5.13]. And the third was that according to Luke, who wrote for those who were from the Gentiles, the gospel that was praised by Paul. And after them all, that according to John.[7]

Augustine, writing at around 400 CE, places the Gospels in this same order, and is explicit that this is regarded as the order of composition:

> So these four evangelists, well-known throughout the entire world (and perhaps they are four because of this, since there are four parts of the world, through the whole of which, they have proclaimed, in a certain manner by the very sacrament of their own number, that the church of Christ has spread) are regarded to have written in this order: first Matthew, then Mark, third Luke, and last John. Hence, there is one order to them in learning and preaching, and another in writing (*De Consensu Evangelistarum* 1.3).

Clement of Alexandria, on the other hand, wrote as following:

> And, again in the same books [*Hypotyoseis* 6], Clement has inserted a tradition from the primitive elders with regard to the order of the Gospels as follows: he said that those Gospels were written first which included the genealogies, and that the Gospel according to Mark came into being in this manner...[8]

The Gospels 'which included the genealogies' are Matthew and Luke (Mt. 1.1-17; Lk. 3.23-38). Thus we have competing traditions, one that places Mark second (Origen, Augustine) and one that places Mark third (Clement). This state of affairs is interesting. It is an annoyance to adherents of the Griesbach Theory, who are keen to stress that the evidence from Clement provides support for their theory, but who have to acknowledge that there is this contradictory witness in Origen. But

---

7.   Origen, quoted by Eusebius, *Ecclesiastical History* 6.25. 'The gospel that was praised by Paul' is a reference to 2 Cor. 8.18. It was thought that Paul was here referring to Luke's Gospel.

8.   Eusebius, *Ecclesiastical History* 6.14.5-7.

further, it tends to confirm the notion that, for the earliest writers, Matt-haean Priority was a reflex of the (for them) related fact that Matthew was directly apostolic, whereas Mark and Luke were only indirectly apostolic. Priority is accorded to the Gospel penned by the tax-collec-tor. Either of the Gospels composed by companions of the apostles, Mark or Luke, may have been third. In other words, we have to treat the patristic evidence with great caution—their agendas and assump-tions in attempting to calculate priority are very different from ours.

Before we leave the question of the patristic evidence, we should note one final key piece of evidence. While it is indeed true that there is unanimity about Matthaean Priority among those who commit them-selves on the order of the Synoptics, it also needs to be noticed that our earliest testimony on synoptic traditions, from Papias, the bishop of Hierapolis (early to mid second century) does not, as far as we can tell, give any support to Matthaean Priority. In the quotations given to us by the fourth-century church historian Eusebius, Papias is quoting his own source, 'the Elder', who apparently mentions both that Mark is an inter-preter of Peter and that Matthew compiled 'the logia' (reports, oracles) in Hebrew, but in the extant passages there is no statement of relative priority.[9]

The patristic evidence, therefore, is not marked enough to encourage us to disregard the overwhelming internal evidence for Markan Priority. Just as we would have to test the student's accusation of plagiarism by looking carefully at the internal evidence presented by the essay in which the alleged plagiarism had taken place, so too it is important for critical scholars to pay careful attention to the internal evidence of the Gospels. And just as we would want to know why the student had made the accusation, we are keen to know the origins of the external evidence about the Gospels. Here it seems that the fathers were more concerned with the 'who' than they were with the 'when' of Gospel composition; and when they did pronounce on the 'when', there are some disagreements over the all-important relative order of Mark and

---

9.   On Papias, see n. 1 above. I have left to one side here the traditions about John's Gospel, also regarded by the fathers as directly apostolic. It seems that here there was an unassailable tradition from early on that it was written relatively late, the kind of tradition apparently lacking for the Synoptics. But again one can see the importance for the fathers of direct, apostolic authorship in that some canonical orders placed John second rather than fourth, and this in spite of the traditions that it was written after Matthew, Mark and Luke.

Luke, key to the Griesbachian scholars, who, on the whole, are so keen to value patristic testimony. Thus where our earliest witness is (as far as we can tell) noncommittal and where our later evidence shows such a clear desire to give priority to the Gospel it thought written by an apostle, and all this in contradiction with the weight of the internal evidence, it will be most prudent to continue to treat the Patristic witness with a pinch of salt.

Summary

- The patristic evidence provides support for Matthaean Priority and it needs to be taken seriously. However, the Fathers were more concerned with the question of the authorship of the Gospels than they were with relative dates. Matthew was thought to have been written by the apostle. When it came to the Gospels bearing the non-apostolic names Mark and Luke, the patristic consensus breaks down and there is disagreement over which Gospel came third. Furthermore, our earliest evidence, Papias, does not tell us either way. Critical scholars will inevitably prefer the overwhelming internal evidence.

8. *Conclusion*

We will take the best route through the maze if we decide firmly in favour of Markan Priority. This is for the following reasons:

(a) *Mark as the middle term*: It was the conclusion of our last chapter, which made a survey of the data, that the key Synoptic fact is that Mark is the middle term. Both in matters of order and wording, Matthew and Luke often agree with Mark. It is less usual for Matthew and Luke to agree with each other against Mark. The two common ways for this to be explained have been Markan Priority (the majority) or Markan Posteriority (a minority). In other words, Mark may be first, and used by both Matthew and Luke; or Mark may be third, so using Matthew and Luke. There are several indications that Markan Priority is the preferable means of explaining the data, including the following.

(b)   *Omissions and additions:*
- Some of the material not in Mark makes better sense on the assumption that it has been added by Matthew and/or Luke than on the assumption that it has been omitted by Mark.
- The material unique to Mark makes better sense as material omitted by Matthew and Luke than it does as material added by Mark.
- If Mark has only added the material that is unique to him, then his Gospel becomes an anomaly in early Christianity, with relatively little contact with oral tradition in comparison with Matthew, Luke, Thomas and others.
- The relationship between the omissions and additions does not make for a coherent picture of Markan redaction: the addition of banal clarificatory additions is not consonant with the generally enigmatic tone of the Gospel.

(c)   *Harder readings*: It is more straightforward to see Mark as the source for Matthew and Luke than to see it redacting them in its difficult passages.

(d)   *Dates*: In so far as there are any internal indications of date in the Synoptics, they suggest that Matthew and Luke are later than Mark.

(e)   *Editorial fatigue*: The most decisive indicator of Markan Priority is evidence that Matthew and Luke made characteristic changes in the early part of pericopae where they were rewriting Mark, lapsing into the wording of their source later in the same pericopae, so producing an inconsistency or an incoherence that betrayed their knowledge of Mark.

One apparently major witness to the opposing theory of Matthean Priority needs to be taken seriously, the patristic evidence, but we cannot help noticing that their judgment was influenced by what was to them a key element, the idea that Matthew was composed by the apostle of that name. When it came to the Gospels bearing the non-apostolic names Mark and Luke, the patristic consensus breaks down and there is disagreement over which Gospel came third. Furthermore, our earliest evidence, Papias, does not tell us either way.

Though a decisive and important step, the all-important postulation of Markan Priority will not, however, take us all the way through the maze. In particular, we need to ask the next logical question: Did

Matthew and Luke use Mark independently of one another or did one of them also know the other? And if Matthew and Luke used Mark independently, how do we explain the origin of the non-Markan material that they share, namely the Double Tradition? We will need to think, in other words, about what kind of literary relationship will best explain all the agreements between Matthew and Luke. This question is a vital one for Synoptic studies and we will consider it in detail in Chapters 5 and 6. But let us not hurry away from the topic of Markan Priority too quickly, for its interest does not consist only in the extent to which it solves one element of the Synoptic Problem. The theory has huge relevance for New Testament study. Next, then, we will explore the ramifications of Markan Priority, in historical, theological, text-critical and redaction-critical terms. It is time to have a look at the role Markan Priority plays in New Testament scholarship.

Chapter 4

BUILDING ON MARKAN PRIORITY

1. *Introduction*

Having touched on the fascination of engaging in Synoptic study
(Chapter 1), and having surveyed the data (Chapter 2) and found a
compelling explanation for some of it in the theory of Markan Priority
(Chapter 3), it is time to consider the relevance of Markan Priority for
the study of the New Testament more broadly. For this is a theory that
has been honoured by time, and one of the reasons that it is held in
such high esteem in the academy is its explanatory power. Markan
Priority helps to make sense of so much of what we see in early Christianity, the Gospels and Jesus. It has been an indispensable prerequisite
of much that has taken place in New Testament scholarship and we
should not let this pass by without comment. There are several ways in
which the theory has helped scholars to reflect profitably on the biblical
text. We will deal with them under the following headings: redaction-
criticism, the study of the historical Jesus and Christian origins and
textual criticism.

2. *Redaction-Criticism*

The theory of Markan Priority has been at the heart of redaction-
criticism, one of the most important methods for studying the Gospels
developed in the previous half-century. Broadly speaking, redaction-
criticism might be defined as the study of the tendencies, nature and
distinctive emphases of a text with a view to ascertaining the theological and literary standpoint of its author. On the whole redaction-criticism eschews interest in the oral origin of units of tradition (pericopae)
that make up the Gospels (more the preserve of *form-criticism*) in order
to concentrate attention on the process by which the evangelists created
their books. The focus is clearly on the authors of each Gospel. For

convenience, the authors are usually called Matthew, Mark and Luke, but without our necessarily thinking that the original authors of these books bore these names.

Redaction-criticism both assumes and builds on the theory of Markan Priority in several ways. First, in assuming Markan Priority, some of the key works of redaction-criticism have looked at Mark without making reference to Matthew and Luke. In other words, it is assumed that Mark was working without knowledge of any other gospel, but was the first to draw together traditional materials about Jesus into a coherent, written whole—his is the first gospel not only in that it was the source of Matthew and Luke but also in the sense that he was the originator of the genre, the first to write this kind of life of Jesus that culminated in an account of his Passion and resurrection.

The task for the redaction-critic of Mark is therefore to find a coherent and plausible explanation of how Mark redacted the materials at his disposal, asking how the distinctive features of his text might be explained by the theological viewpoint of its original author. The quest has generated some fascinating proposals—redaction-criticism of Mark has become something of a rich industry within biblical scholarship. Perhaps Mark, for example, is the first person to forge together into a coherent whole the Pauline *kerygma* (preaching) of the crucified Christ with the traditions that were circulating concerning Jesus' life and ministry, beginning his Gospel with accounts of Jesus' teaching ability and healing power and, as the story progresses, taking the reader on a journey, 'the way of the Lord', towards a kingdom constituted by the cross of a crucified Messiah.

The obvious difficulty that redaction-criticism of Mark introduces is the question of Mark's source material. On the assumption of Markan Priority, we do not have any of Mark's sources extant and one of the dangers in redaction-criticism of Mark is the potential circularity of reconstructing Mark's sources on the basis of a reconstruction of what one thinks Mark might have done with them. On the Griesbach Theory, one does not have the same difficulty, for Mark is redacting his Gospel on the basis of Matthew and Luke, omitting, reworking and entwining sources that we have in front of us. But this, unfortunately, is one of the genuine problems that scholars continue to confront in coming to terms with the Griesbach Theory, the lack of a convincing redaction-critical explanation for the choices that Mark makes, a lack that competes with so many plausible and intriguing studies of Mark that work on the assumption that he was responsible for the origin of the Gospel genre as we know it.

But the anxiety about our inability to compare Mark with extant sources has produced different results that both build on and react against redaction-criticism of Mark. While the newer, emerging discipline of narrative-criticism pronounces itself firmly uninterested in the matter of sources, focusing purely on the individual text at hand, narrative-criticism of Mark nevertheless aligns itself with redaction-criticism of Mark in avoiding comparison with the other Synoptics. It is probably no coincidence that Mark has particularly lent itself to narrative-critical analysis given the legacy of redaction-criticism that bases itself on the priority of Mark, likewise not having to be concerned about comparison between Mark the other Synoptics.

What then of redaction-criticism of Matthew and Luke? It too has been developed on the assumption of Markan Priority, but in different ways from redaction-criticism of Mark. For here we have one of the sources of Matthew and Luke on the table in front of us ready for analysis. It is one of the most clear and straightforward ways in which study of the Synoptic Problem interacts with Gospel studies more generally. Many of the insights that have been gleaned from the study of Matthew and Luke are the product of comparison between Matthew and Mark and between Luke and Mark. Where one can watch what a writer is doing with a source, one can gain a much clearer profile of that writer. It is true on both the level of the overarching designs of Matthew and Luke and on the detailed level of their individual sentences—the redaction-critic analyses Matthew and Luke in the light of the assumption that they were using Mark, an assumption that tends towards the notion that Matthew and Luke were both attempts to 'fix' Mark, to supplement, rewrite and correct (what they saw as) its inadequacies while at the same time drawing on it.

As we have seen already, Matthew and Luke both incorporate the basic structure of Mark, John the Baptist—Temptation—teaching and healing ministry in Galilee—Passion in Jerusalem, but both appear to find this structure in need of major supplementation. Thus both Matthew and Luke rework Mark by adding Birth Narratives at the beginning of their respective Gospels, and resurrection appearances at the end. Perhaps then, like many a modern reader, they found Mark to be lacking—rather shorter than one might expect—beginning too late and ending too early and in the middle missing many of the matters that might be regarded as essential, the Lord's Prayer for example, or the Beatitudes. Indeed Matthew and Luke both feature a great deal more sayings material than does Mark—proportionally more space is taken up in both Matthew and Luke with teaching material than it is in Mark, something that itself substantially alters the picture of Jesus we receive from Mark.

On the assumption of Markan Priority, then, the first readers of Mark found it to be inadequate. And this is true not only of questions of structure and content—the questions concerning what Mark did not include—but also on the more detailed level of its individual pericopae and sentences within them. Its language is somewhat colloquial. Some might even call it sloppy. There are broken sentences, the obsessively frequent use of 'and' or 'and immediately' and the regular use of the historic present, 'he says', 'he goes', 'he enters'. For both of the later evangelists, this style wanted some substantial modification. Both make major changes and Luke in particular recasts Mark in a much more 'literary' Greek style, omitting all of Mark's historic presents and eliminating many of the regular 'and's.

The key matter, though, is to see that Matthew and Luke differed from Mark in theology and Christology. Their conceptions of what God, Jesus and the disciples were like overlapped with Mark's conception but were not identical to it. Thus, for example, we might remember that Matthew apparently altered Mark's comment that 'Jesus could do no mighty work' in Nazareth (6.6) to a statement that 'Jesus did not do there many mighty works' (Mt. 13.58). Likewise, we might recall that the gradual healing of the blind man, no doubt seen to be implying some limit on Jesus' power (Mk 8.22-26) is omitted in Matthew and Luke. Nor, again, is Jesus so enigmatic in Matthew and Luke. The elements of secrecy recede into the background and the edge is taken off that darkly ironic Markan portrait (see above, pp. 64-65). Where there are questions in Mark, there is explication in both Matthew and Luke. Consider, for example, the following passage:

Matthew 17.9-13	*Mark 9.9-13*
9. And as they were coming down the mountain, Jesus commanded them, 'Tell no one the vision, until the Son of man is raised from the dead'.	9. And as they were coming down the mountain, he charged them to tell no one what they had seen, until the Son of man should have risen from the dead.

	10. So they kept the matter to themselves, questioning what the rising from the dead meant.
10. And the disciples asked him, 'Then why do the scribes say that first Elijah must come?' 11. He replied, 'Elijah does come, and he is to restore all things;	11. And they asked him, 'Why do the scribes say that first Elijah must come?' 12. And he said to them, 'Elijah does come first to restore all things; and how is it written of the Son of man, that he should suffer many things and be treated with contempt?
12. but I tell you that Elijah has already come, and they did not know him, but did to him whatever they pleased. So also the Son of man will suffer at their hands'. 13. Then the disciples understood that he was speaking to them of John the Baptist.	13. But I tell you that Elijah has come, and they did to him whatever they pleased, as it is written of him'.

This example falls into the 'not quite Triple Tradition' category (see above, pp. 48-50, occasions where material is common to Matthew and Mark alone or to Mark and Luke alone). Typically, Mark's text is allusive: it implies a knowledge both of the Hebrew Bible and of itself, leaving the reader to do a good deal of the work. Here, we are expected to have read the earlier part of the Gospel carefully, noticing that John the Baptist's appearance resembled that of Elijah (Mk 1.6; cf. 2 Kgs 1.8) and that the story of John the Baptist, Herod and Herodias is fashioned after and alludes to the stories of Elijah, Ahab and Jezebel (Mk 6.14-29; 1 Kgs 17-22). Now careful readers of Mark who know their Hebrew Bible will at this stage in Mark make a link, encouraged by the saying of Jesus here recorded. They will see that Elijah has indeed come, in John the Baptist, and that this confirms the messianic identity of Jesus that the disciples are now beginning to perceive (8.30). Further—and this is the key element—the sharp reader is expected to see that Jesus will meet an end that is similar to that of John—'they did to him whatever they pleased, as it is written of him' and so too the Son of Man will 'suffer many things', also as 'it is written'. The reader of this passage in Mark, who reads in the context of both the Gospel and the Hebrew Bible, is left reflecting on the relationship between John the Baptist, the scriptures, Jesus' identity, suffering, messiahship and the disciples' perception.

Now Matthew, whose account differs little from Mark's, nevertheless adds a concluding comment not paralleled in Mark: 'Then the disciples understood…' This is typical of Matthew. He knows his Scriptures and he has been reading Mark and getting to know the book for some time. He sees what Mark is doing here but is concerned that his readers might miss it. So the allusive Mark, which prefers to keep things as subtle as possible, gets reworked when it is absorbed into Matthew, where matters are stated strongly and unambiguously. The same thing happens again when Matthew is redacting the Markan incident concerning bread on the boat (Mk 8.13-21//Mt. 16.4-12). The Markan account is bizarre and somewhat difficult to fathom, ending on an open question, addressed no doubt to the reader as well as to the disciples in the Gospel: 'Do you not yet understand… ?' Equally as typically, Matthew by contrast adds one of his clarificatory sentences, 'Then they understood that he did not tell them to beware of the leaven of bread, but of the teaching of the Pharisees and Sadducees' (16.12). Where Mark has questions, and disciples who cannot fathom the answers, Matthew has clear statements, and disciples who understand.

Thus Matthew, Mark's first reader, perceives what Mark is doing, but decides to make it absolutely clear for his readers. Indeed one of the reasons for the current scholarly fascination with Mark is, no doubt, that this is a text that leaves the interpreter with plenty of work to do.

Let us have a look at another example of the way in which redaction-criticism of Matthew and Luke can work within a single pericope. Earlier we noticed some interesting differences in the story of the stilling of the storm. Now let us explore the differences in a little more detail.

Matthew 8.25-26	Mark 4.38-39	Luke 8.24-25
And the disciples, having approached him, awoke him saying, 'Lord, save! We are perishing!' * Then, having got up, he rebuked the winds and the sea,	And they awake him and say to him, 'Teacher, do you not care that we are perishing?' And having awoken, he rebuked the wind and said to the sea, 'Be silent! Be muzzled!' And the wind ceased, and there was a great calm.	And having approached him they awoke him saying, 'Master Master, we are perishing!' And having awoken, he rebuked the wind and the raging of the water. And they ceased, and there was a calm.
and there was a great calm'.		

*And he says to them, 'Why are you afraid, ye of little faith?'	And he said to them, 'Why are you so afraid? Have you still no faith?'	And he said to them, 'Where is your faith?'

Where Mark's Jesus is harsh towards the disciples ('Have you still no faith?') and the disciples have no respect for Jesus ('Do you not care...?'), both Matthew and Luke have a little more reverence. In Matthew they have characteristically 'little faith' (cf. Mt. 14.31; 16.8), not none, and in Luke the question is 'Where is your faith?' as if this is but a temporary lapse. And the insulting question 'Do you not care...?' is omitted by both. This is the kind of pattern that one finds throughout.

The redaction-critic will also notice places where the style of Matthew and Luke characteristically differs from that of Mark. Luke, ever the master of writing a lively story, adds the doubled vocative 'Master Master' just as, elsewhere, Jesus says 'Martha Martha' (Lk. 10.41), 'Simon Simon' (Lk. 22.31) and 'Saul Saul' (Acts 9.4). Matthew, often regarded as the most liturgical of the Gospels, has the disciples sounding like they are in church chanting a confession, 'Lord, save!' just as elsewhere those who 'approach' Jesus say 'Lord, have mercy!' (17.15).

Redaction-criticism is not very difficult once one gets used to practising it. Indeed this kind of redaction-criticism is a lot of fun and gives students with even the most basic knowledge of the Gospels a feeling of empowerment as they practise a form of exegesis directly involving the biblical text. It is one of the best ways of becoming familiar with the Synoptic Gospels generally and the Synoptic Problem specifically. For those who have not practised it themselves before, here is how to go about it:

(a) Get hold of a Synopsis of the Gospels and start looking at parallel passages.

(b) Choose a passage, preferably from the 'Triple Tradition' (occurring in all three Synoptics), and begin to find the similarities and differences between Matthew, Mark and Luke. One of the best ways of doing this is by photocopying the relevant page in your Synopsis and then doing some colouring—see the suggested scheme above in Chapter 2.

(c) Focus on the differences between the Gospels and attempt to find places where Matthew or Luke do the same thing elsewhere in their Gospels. This is easier to do these days because of the advent of useful electronic Bible search tools,[1] but the more familiar you become with the Gospels, the more you will be able to think of the parallels without having to look them up. In the example above, for instance, it would be straightforward to look for other occurrences of the term 'little faith' in Matthew.

(d) Find an explanation for the kinds of change you have isolated. In the example above, you might notice that the disciples in Matthew appear to be those of 'little faith' and that this contrasts to their total lack of faith in Mark.

As one becomes more and more familiar with the Gospels, one finds redaction-criticism based on the assumption of Markan Priority easier and easier to do. It is a popular discipline and on the whole it has been extraordinarily successful, so much so in fact that it is now sometimes said that it functions itself as an argument for Markan Priority, the logic being that redaction-criticism has been so fruitful that it establishes the usefulness and plausibility of the starting point, the assumption of Markan Priority. This is a difficult proposition to test, though, because so many works have been written assuming Markan Priority that it generates a kind of momentum of its own, and there is no counterbalance. Nevertheless, it also needs to be said that so far Griesbachian scholars are not generally regarded as having made a strong enough case for the reinvention of redaction-criticism on the assumption that Mark used Matthew and Luke. Perhaps in time the demonstration will be forthcoming—but they have got a lot of stubborn academic minds to change and victory does not look imminent. For the time being at least, this kind of redaction-criticism based on Markan Priority will continue to be practised extensively and profitably by Gospel exegetes.

Summary

- *Redaction-Criticism:* The process by which scholars analyse the tendencies, nature and distinctive emphases of the Synoptic Gospels with a view to ascertaining the literary and theological

---

1. I have gathered together several such tools, all available for free on the Internet on a site called *All-in-One Biblical Resources Search* (created November 1999), http://www.ntgateway.com/multibib.htm.

standpoint of their authors. In study of Mark, Matthew and Luke, the theory of Markan Priority has been key.

- *Mark's Gospel*: Because of the theory of Markan Priority, most scholars have assumed that Mark was the first writer to forge together the traditional materials about Jesus into a narrative framework with a specific agenda. The Gospel genre was born here. For many, the birth of the genre was the result of Mark's attempt to couch the Jesus tradition in the framework of a Passion that is anticipated from the beginning, subordinating the materials about Jesus' life to a narrative of suffering and death.

- *Matthew and Luke*: Markan Priority helps us to notice the extent to which Matthew and Luke are attempts to 'fix' Mark, to fill it out by adding birth and infancy tales at the beginning, fuller resurrection stories at the end and lots of fresh teaching material in between. Direct comparison between Mark and Matthew and between Mark and Luke quickly reveals each evangelist's distinctive emphases, encouraging us to extrapolate to an hypothesis about the evangelists' literary and theological agendas.

3. *Historical Jesus and Christian Origins*

Markan Priority has also been the cornerstone of a great deal of work on the historical Jesus and Christian origins. After all, it is in the job description of a sound historian to sift sources, looking in particular for the earliest material and the most primitive traditions. If Mark is first, and if the Triple Tradition material is directly derived by Matthew and Luke from Mark, then it follows that the historian will want to spend more time—for the triple tradition material at least—with Mark than with Matthew and Luke. And this, on the whole, is the course that study of the historical Jesus and Christian origins has taken. When looking at Triple Tradition pericopae, Mark is accorded an exalted position.

The special place that Markan Priority has in historical Jesus work is largely justified. It is natural, for example, for scholars to spend more time looking at Mark's account of the Passion of Jesus (Mk 14–16) than at, say, Matthew's largely derivative version (Mt. 26–28). Or there is a natural tendency in research into Jesus' parables to prefer the

Markan versions of Triple Tradition parables to the Matthean and Lukan versions derived from them. Or on Christology, we might note the differences between the Synoptics and extrapolate to an hypothesis about the development of views about Jesus. We looked at a good example of this in our first chapter above, the story of the Rich Young Ruler in which Matthew's account differs at just the point where there is potential ambiguity about Jesus' divinity (Mt. 19.16-17//Mk 10.17-18//Lk. 18.18-19, pp. 25-26 above), something which, on the assumption of Markan Priority, is due to Matthew's deliberate removal of ambiguity and embarrassment.

Nevertheless, it does need to be added that the privilege accorded to Mark in the study of the historical Jesus and Christian origins can easily become excessive. Since here we touch on a point that is seldom mentioned, and since it will also be important later when we investigate the Double Tradition, it is worth pausing for a moment to consider this carefully. The basic concern is this: while it seems clear that Markan Priority is a fine working principle for historical enquiry, the obsession with positing it above all else has sometimes resulted in a kind of mechanical adherence that negates the possibility that Matthew and Luke, in their rewriting of Mark, might also have been interacting with oral traditions independent of Mark. We should ever be wary of the assumption that 'earliest' is necessarily best, that the text closest in time to the events being related is always and inevitably the most reliable. We only need to think of our own distance from leading events in the twentieth century to see the point. We might well write a better biography of Elvis Presley or John Lennon today than anyone was able to write in 1981, even though we might be directly dependent on that biography of 1981 for some of our material. It is not just that more research uncovers more sources. It is also a question of perspective and context—sometimes the years intervening between events and accounts of them can generate a more critical, a more nuanced perspective. The analogy is not perfect, of course, but it does help us to remember not to allow an undue obsession with Matthew's and Luke's literary dependence on Mark to affect our historical Jesus scholarship.

The point can be illustrated with a general example and a specific one. First, the general example. It is worth noting that Matthew's Jesus is a much more blatantly Jewish Jesus than is Mark's. Now in this, it seems likely that Matthew is effectively closer to the historical Jesus than is Mark. For it is a consensus of good historical Jesus scholarship of the last generation or so that we need to take seriously Jesus' Judaism and Jewish context. If this is right, then one of the things that Matthew is doing in his Gospel is not just to 'Judaize' Jesus but to 're-Judaize' the Jesus of Mark's Gospel. Perhaps it was one of the things that led Matthew to write this Gospel, with its desire to draw from the treasure-chest both 'the new' and 'the old' (Mt. 13.52). The evangelist found much in Mark's Gospel that was of great worth to him, but he was concerned about its general Gentile bias in which Jesus sits lightly to the Law.

Second, a specific example. In order to understand this, we need to remember that, from the earliest days of the Christian movement, oral traditions of Jesus' sayings and deeds were circulating. The first Christians no doubt told one another, as well as new converts, about the Jesus story and Jesus' sayings. The apostle Paul witnesses to this—he reminds the readers of his letters of several of Jesus' sayings (for example 1 Cor. 7.12 on divorce; 9.14 on mission; and 11.23-26 on the Eucharist). Now it is hardly likely that oral traditions of the Jesus story died out as soon as the evangelists committed them to papyrus. Indeed the later evidence shows us that oral traditions of the Jesus story continued for a considerable time after the Canonical Gospels first became known. Thus when Matthew and Luke were writing their Gospels, it seems highly likely that they will have interacted with oral traditions of some of the same material that they found in their primary literary source, Mark. This will mean that on occasion, Matthew and Luke will inevitably bear witness to different, sometimes more original versions of Jesus material than the versions found in Mark, their literary source.

Since the point is seldom seen and might not be immediately grasped by people immersed in purely literary ways of thinking, I will attempt to illustrate it from our own culture. Most of us will be familiar with popular children's stories like *Snow White* and *Aladdin*, which continue to be told and retold in multiple different versions with local variations, expansions and colour. Many of us will also know the Disney versions of these stories. Now when Disney produced their version of *Snow White* in 1937, other retellings of the *Snow White* story did not immediately die a death. Many later versions of *Snow White* were strongly influenced by the Disney version, but the latter did not obliterate other ways of telling the same story. So too, after *Aladdin* appeared in 1992, other versions of the *Aladdin* story continued to be told, even though many versions now tended to depict the genie along the same lines as in the Disney film. In other words, a new, apparently definitive version of a story even in our own culture strongly influences but does not obliterate other versions of the same story in subsequent retellings.

It is likely that Matthew's and Luke's treatment of Mark worked along similar lines. Since they were already familiar with other versions of some of the stories that they subsequently encountered in literary form in Mark, they redacted Mark in interaction with these oral traditions. But how can we be sure that this is the case? Is there anything more than just general likelihood? What we need is a good example that will illustrate the point. We are lucky that we have an example of a pericope that we will suspect to have been particularly prone to influence from oral tradition, the words at the institution of the Eucharist. This is a useful pericope in this context because we will expect passages that formed part of early Christian liturgy to have been well known, repeated in differing versions across a wide geographical stretch. Thus this is the kind of passage where we will expect to see Luke showing signs of knowledge of a different or more primitive than the one appearing in Mark. Have a look again at the Synopsis:

Matthew 26.27-28	Mark 14.23-24	Luke 22.20	1 Corinthians 11.25
And after he had taken the cup and given thanks, he gave it to them saying, 'Drink from it, all. For this is my blood of the covenant which is shed for many for the forgiveness of sins'.	And after he had taken the cup and given thanks, he gave it to them and they all drank from it. And he said to them, 'This is my blood of the covenant which is shed for many'.	And likewise (he took) the cup after supper, saying, 'This cup is the new covenant in my blood, which is shed for you'.	And likewise (he took) the cup after supper, saying, 'This cup is the new covenant in my blood. Do this, as often as you drink, in my memory'.

What is so interesting about this passage is that Paul's version is very early—the words of institution occur in 1 Corinthians, normally dated to the early fifties, well within a generation of the original event that is being related. Now Luke, in spite of the fact that we know him to have been literarily dependent on Mark, is nevertheless apparently

influenced by something resembling the very early tradition also known
to Paul. Luke, in other words, seems to be rewriting Mark in interaction
with a version of the same story known to him from his oral tradition.[2]
It is possible that Matthew too is reworking Mark in line with a version
of the Eucharistic words more familiar to him. While the words unique
to Matthew, 'for the forgiveness of sins', may simply be the evangelist's own creative addition, it is equally possible that these are words
Matthew has added from his own oral tradition.

In short, observations like this do not compromise the theory of the
literary Priority of Mark, but they do have importance for studying the
history of traditions. It appears to be quite plausible that both Matthew's and Luke's knowledge of oral tradition interacted with and
affected their reading of Mark's Gospel, something that is always
worth bearing in mind when we engage in the study of Christian
origins.

This important qualification having been made, the general point
nevertheless remains absolutely vital, that studies of the historical Jesus
and of early Christian origins will continue to build on the theory of
Markan Priority. Perhaps most important of all, and so a good way to
conclude this section, is the way that Markan Priority helps us to
understand the very origin of the Gospel genre. For if Mark is indeed
the first Gospel, then we inevitably find ourselves reflecting on how
this Gospel was generated. If Matthew and Luke are primarily attempts
to 'fix' Mark, to use it as a backbone but to correct it and fill it out, the
question of the origin of Mark's Gospel presses itself on us forcefully.
Is there anything in the book's structure, theology, outlook, appearance, that helps us to understand what caused the first evangelist to
produce what we are now used to calling a 'Gospel'? The question
might sound odd to us because we are so used to the idea of lives of
Jesus of the kind Mark was the first to write. But it seems to have been
by no means self-evident in the first Christian generation that a Gospel
book of this kind was necessary or desirable—at least 30 years, and
probably more, separate Mark's Gospel from the events it is relating.

The fascinating thing about Mark's Gospel is that it does yield up
answers to our questions about the origin of the Gospel genre. There
are three interesting features of Mark's Gospel that give us clues:

---

    2.   Michael Goulder, however, argues that Luke is dependent here on 1 Corin-
thians and not on the oral tradition also known to Paul (*Luke: A New Paradigm*,
ch. 4).

(a) there is a marked element of secrecy, enigma and mystery connected with Jesus' identity and activity; (b) in spite of this, key elements in the narrative strongly affirm that Jesus is Messiah and Son of God; and (c) Jesus' messiahship appears to be understood in line with a major stress on his suffering and death. A popular and plausible scholarly explanation of these striking features is as follows. Mark's Gospel was generated by the desire to marry the traditional materials the evangelist knew with his own strongly held belief that Jesus was the Messiah, and, furthermore, that the key to and culmination of his Messiahship was suffering and death. Mark's means of stamping this belief on the disparate materials at his disposal, materials that were not always conducive to Mark's interests, was first, a 'mystery' motif and second, a related stress on Jesus' suffering and death.

The mystery motif is a narrative device, a means by which Mark is able to affirm Jesus' messianic identity by placing confessions in the mouths of the narrator (1.1), God (1.11) and demons (1.24; 1.34; 3.11-12), while at the same time most of the characters in the drama—particularly the disciples, on whom Mark places special stress—remain blissfully ignorant of who Jesus is. What Mark seems to have done is to marry his traditions—stories and sayings that were often non-messianic or uninterested in the notion of Jesus' messiahship—with his strongly held belief that Jesus was indeed Messiah. And this marriage is performed by means of the narrative device of irony and enigma. The readers can see what the characters in the drama cannot see. We are allowed to hear God's perspective, the demons' perspective, and the narrator's perspective, but they cannot.

But this is not the whole story—the messiahship of Jesus is nuanced and qualified by Mark in the direction of suffering and death. The first half of the Gospel, in which Jesus' messiahship is established, is subordinated to the second half of the Gospel in which his destiny—suffering and death—is predicted (three times, Mk 8.31; 9.31; 10.31-32), anticipated (Mk 10.35-45; 12.1-12) and then enacted (Mk 14–16). The pivot is the mid-point in the Gospel, the moment when Simon Peter correctly confesses that Jesus is Messiah (Mk 8.29), but fails to accept the key point, that Jesus will suffer, leading to the famous rebuke, 'Get thee behind me Satan!' (Mk 8.31-33). In the end, the disciples never manage to make the vital connection between suffering and Messiahship, but others do. First an unnamed woman 'anoints' Jesus for his 'burial' (Mk 14.1-9; bear in mind that 'Messiah' means 'Anointed') and then, after the Twelve have variously denied, betrayed and fled from Jesus, a group of women replace them as the true disciples at the cross, having 'followed' him and 'ministered' to him from the beginning (Mk 15.40-41).

Mark is all about a Messiah who suffers. It is the relentless theme of his Gospel, increasing in intensity as the narrative reaches its goal. It seems clear that the writer of this Gospel had an ulterior motive. Many see him as in the legacy of the apostle Paul, for whom the crucified Messiah was the heart of 'the gospel' message (e.g. Gal. 6.14). Accordingly, given the mystery motif connected with Jesus' messiahship, especially in the first half of the Gospel, and given Mark's stress on Jesus as a messiah who was crucified in the second half, it seems likely that the Gospel genre originated in Mark's attempt to take Paul's message and marry it to the traditions about Jesus' life and death that he knew. Or, to use somewhat old-fashioned, technical terminology, he has generated his Gospel by 'Paulinizing the *kerygma*'.[3]

Without the theory of Markan Priority, a theory that emerges directly from the careful study of the Synoptic Problem, none of these reflections would be possible. We would have to paint a radically different picture of Christian origins. There seems little doubt, then, that the Synoptic Problem in general and Markan Priority in particular have an enormous impact on the way we do New Testament scholarship. It is a useful reminder that having some idea of the Synoptic Problem is simply indispensable for reflection on the identity of the historical Jesus and the development of Christian doctrine. One should not be persuaded by the rhetoric of those who say that the Synoptic Problem is boring or irrelevant!

Summary

- Markan Priority has caused scholars of the historical Jesus to pay special attention to his accounts. In historical Jesus

3.   Discussions of the Gospel genre abound, and various suggestions have been made about ancient parallels for the Gospel genre. My point here is, not withstanding that there are helpful parallels in other ancient materials, these are the factors that probably led Mark to produce what most agree to be the first 'Gospel'. For discussion of the secrecy motif in Mark, a good starting point is C.M. Tuckett (ed.), *The Messianic Secret* (London: SPCK; Philadelphia: Fortress Press Press, 1983).

research, Mark is therefore of key importance. Nevertheless, it also needs to be noticed that literary priority is not everything, and reflection on parallel Synoptic accounts sometimes leads to the observation that Matthew and Luke may have interacted not only with Mark but also with oral traditions as they composed their Gospels.

- The theory of Markan Priority encourages fruitful investigation of the origin of the Gospel genre. It is plausible to think of Mark as the first author to compose a gospel, gathering together the traditions at his disposal and subordinating materials about Jesus' life to a narrative focused on the Passion, so stamping his book with a stress on a Pauline theology of a suffering messiah.

4. *Textual Criticism*

This is the study of the actual physical manuscripts that are our witnesses to the text of the New Testament, and it can interact with the theory of Markan Priority in some fascinating ways. For if we place Mark first, then Matthew and Luke become two of Mark's earliest editors. Like later scribes copying out the text of Mark they inevitably make corrections, additions, omissions and changes. And the changes Matthew and Luke made as they rewrote Mark's material are especially interesting in that they often parallel changes made by scribes copying Mark. Sometimes this will be because the Markan scribes have been influenced by the very changes that Matthew and Luke made in their 'versions' of Mark; sometimes it will be because the thought processes that were influencing Matthew and Luke will have influenced Markan scribes too; and sometimes it will be both factors, interacting with one another.

To understand the point, we need to remember that we do not possess the original autographs of the Gospels, but we work, instead, from the many manuscript 'witnesses'. One of the text critic's key tasks is the attempt to reconstruct the original text of each Gospel as accurately as possible on the basis of careful analysis of these manuscripts, a job that is particularly interesting in the case of the Synoptic Gospels, where the material is often so similar. It is clear, for example, that scribes who copied texts of Mark were often influenced by the parallel texts in Matthew and Luke. They 'assimilated' to the more familiar text, harmonizing to the version that they knew best. Consider the following text, for example:

Matthew 12.3-4	Mark 2.25-26	Luke 6.3-4
He said to them, 'Have you not read what David did, when he was hungry, and those who were with him: how he entered the house of God	And he said to them, 'Have you never read what David did, when he was in need and was hungry, he and those who were with him: how he entered the house of God, *when Abiathar was high priest,*	And Jesus answered, 'Have you not read what David did when he was hungry, he and those who were with him: how he entered the house of God,
and ate the bread of the Presence, which it was not lawful for him to eat nor for those who were with him, but only for the priests?	and ate the bread of the Presence, which it is not lawful for any but the priests to eat, and also gave it to those who were with him?'	and took and ate the bread of the Presence, which it is not lawful for any but the priests to eat, and also gave it to those with him?'

The words in italics here, 'when Abiathar was high priest' (Mk 2.26), are an error. The incident related (1 Sam. 21.1-6) involves not Abiathar but his father Ahimelech. On the assumption of Markan Priority, Matthew and Luke realized this and omitted the words (for there are no manuscripts of Matthew and Luke that feature the words 'when Abiathar was high priest'). It is of interest that certain scribes of Mark made the same excision, perhaps under the influence of the more familiar versions of the account in Matthew and Luke, perhaps (like them) perceiving the error. Both Codex Bezae ('D'), an important manuscript of the Gospels and Acts produced in about 400, and the Freer Gospels (or Codex Washingtonianus, 'W'), an important manuscript of the Gospels copied in the late fourth century, do not feature these words in their copy of Mark.

In cases like this what one really needs is a three-dimensional Synopsis.[4] Normally, we look at two-dimensional synopses that show us how critical, reconstructed texts of the Gospels relate to one another.

---

4.   I am grateful to my colleague David Parker for some of these observations (*The Living Text of the Gospels* [Cambridge: Cambridge University Press, 1997], ch. 7).

This is what we have done in each example in this book so far. But one of the difficulties with this standard approach is that it can lull one into a false sense of security about the state of the text of the respective Gospels, and in many cases something more elaborate would be more appropriate. Perhaps, one day, someone will invent an electronic synopsis that enables one to view not just critical texts of Matthew, Mark and Luke in parallel but also different texts of each of the Gospels, layered on top of one another. In the meantime, we can at least add an extra column to our threefold synopsis to illustrate the point a little further. Here columns 1, 2 and 4 represent the usual 'critical text' of the Synoptics on which we have relied elsewhere in this book. This critical text is a reconstruction, the best approximation that the experts can make to what the original versions of the New Testament looked like. Column 3 shows how the same text looks in Codex Bezae, the early manuscript of the Gospels mentioned above.

Matthew 8.3 (Critical Text)	Mark 1.41 (Critical Text)	Mark 1.41 (Codex Bezae)	Luke 5.13 (Critical Text)
And	And *having been moved with compassion*, and	And *having been moved with anger*, and	And
having stretched out the hand, he touched him, saying, 'I will; be clean'.	having stretched out his hand, he touched (him), and says to him, 'I will; be clean'.	having stretched out his hand, he touched him, and says to him, 'I will; be clean'.	having stretched out the hand, he touched him, saying, 'I will; be clean'.

One of the fascinating elements about the text here is the disagreement over whether to read 'compassion' or 'anger'. Given that the latter is in many ways the more difficult reading—scribes are likely to have preferred the idea of a compassionate Jesus to an angry Jesus—it may be that Codex Bezae has the authentic reading. This is then a different but equally interesting case of textual criticism interacting with the theory of Markan Priority. For here one cannot help thinking that Matthew and Luke are more likely to have changed a text that read 'moved with anger' than they were to have changed a text that read 'moved with compassion', especially as Matthew has that very phrase in a similar context elsewhere (Mt. 20.34). In this example, then, textual criticism helps us to reconstruct the text that may have been in front of Matthew and Luke, and to discover a reason for their mutual omission of words in Mark.

Textual criticism can, then, interact profitably with Synoptic Problem scholarship, and in particular with the theory of Markan Priority. In the story of the Leper, it can help us to speculate on the text of Mark from which Matthew and Luke were working, adding an extra, fascinating dimension to our Synoptic comparison and helping us to remember that when we open the Bible we are looking not at the evangelists' original words but at a modern scholarly reconstruction of what they may have written.

And in our first example, the story of the Cornfield on the Sabbath, text criticism can help us to see how scribes were influenced by Matthew's and Luke's redaction of Mark. This does not necessarily constitute an argument for the Priority of Mark, for it is a fact that scribes of Mark often 'assimilated' to the other Gospels, and especially to Matthew, thus rewriting Mark, largely unconsciously, in the light of the more familiar and much preferred Matthew. But to press this would be to miss the point that Markan scribes are on what we might label a 'trajectory', which begins, on the assumption of Markan Priority, with Matthew's and Luke's rewriting of Mark. Thus Matthew's and Luke's interaction with Mark ultimately changed Mark too. It is arguably a mark of the success of their rewriting of Mark that they so influenced the textual tradition. And in their interaction with Matthew and Luke, such Markan scribes take a position tantamount to correcting Mark, tacitly siding with the later Gospels in their desire to correct and improve it.

Summary

- *Textual criticism*, the study of the manuscripts of the New Testament, reminds us that the differences between Matthew, Mark and Luke are differences between modern, critical texts of the Synoptics, texts that have been reconstructed. It is fascinating and informative to view Markan Priority through the multiple lenses provided by textual criticism. Sometimes we see signs of a text of Mark that perhaps Matthew and Luke also saw; sometimes we see texts of Mark that have been influenced by the changes made by Matthew and Luke.

5. *Conclusion*

Markan Priority remains at the heart of a great deal of New Testament study. Our reflections on Markan Priority have helped us to see just how relevant and valuable the study of the Synoptic Problem has become as a building block for other elements in Gospel scholarship. We have looked in this chapter at three important areas where reflecting on Markan Priority can help us to discuss the New Testament and Christian origins. Let us briefly summarize:

(a)   *Redaction-criticism:* This has been one of the key critical methods in New Testament scholarship, analysing the tendencies, nature and distinctive emphases of the Synoptic Gospels with a view to ascertaining the theological standpoint of their authors. In study of Mark, Matthew and Luke, the theory of Markan Priority has been key:

- *Mark's Gospel*: Because of the theory of Markan Priority, most scholars have assumed that Mark was the first writer to forge together the traditional materials about Jesus into a narrative framework with a specific agenda. The Gospel genre was born here. For many, the birth of the genre was the result of Mark's attempt to couch the Jesus tradition in the framework of a Passion that is anticipated from the beginning, subordinating the materials about Jesus' life to a narrative of suffering and death.
- *Matthew and Luke*: Markan Priority helps us to notice the extent to which Matthew and Luke are attempts to 'fix' Mark, to fill it out by adding birth and infancy tales at the beginning, fuller resurrection stories at the end and lots of fresh teaching material in between. Direct comparison between the Synoptics quickly reveals each evangelist's distinctive emphases, encouraging us to extrapolate to an hypothesis about the evangelists' literary and theological agendas.

(b)   *Historical Jesus and Christian Origins:*

- Markan Priority has caused scholars of the historical Jesus to pay special attention to Mark's accounts. In historical Jesus research, Mark is therefore of key importance. Nevertheless, it also needs to be noticed that literary priority is not everything, and reflection on parallel Synoptic accounts sometimes leads to the observation that Matthew and Luke may have interacted not only with Mark but also with oral traditions as they composed their Gospels.

- The theory of Markan Priority encourages fruitful investigation of the origin of the Gospel genre. It is plausible to think of Mark as the first author to compose a Gospel, gathering together the traditions at his disposal and subordinating materials about Jesus' life to a narrative focused on the Passion, so stamping his book with a stress on a Pauline theology of a suffering Messiah.

(c)   *Textual criticism*: the study of the manuscript tradition of the Gospels reminds us that the differences between Matthew, Mark and Luke are differences between modern, critical texts of the Synoptics, texts that have been reconstructed by means of textual criticism. It is fascinating and informative to view Markan Priority through the multiple lenses provided by textual criticism. Sometimes we see a signs of a text of Mark that perhaps Matthew and Luke also saw; sometimes we see texts of Mark that have been influenced by the changes made by Matthew and Luke.

These are just some of the ways in which we might reflect profitably on the theory of Markan Priority. For our purposes, the most important corollary of our decision in favour of Markan Priority is, however, the one that builds on it to help us understand properly the data for which we have not yet accounted on our way through the maze. Markan Priority has profound implications for how we solve the remainder of the Synoptic Problem. When in Chapter 2 we looked carefully at the data, we divided it up into four major types, Triple Tradition, Double Tradition, Special Matthew and Special Luke. The Triple Tradition material, the pericopae that feature in all three Synoptics, seems to be more than adequately explained by the theory of Markan Priority. In each case, Matthew and Luke are literarily dependent on Mark. Let us turn next, therefore, to the Double Tradition material, the pericopae shared by Matthew and Luke alone.

There are two ways to explain the Double Tradition material by taking for granted and building on Markan Priority. The first of these theories we will look at next, the theory that Matthew and Luke used Mark independently of one another, and thus that they could only have taken over the Double Tradition from another, hitherto undiscovered source. The second theory we will look at in the final chapter, in which we will consider the weaknesses of the Q hypothesis, and build on Markan Priority by suggesting that Luke knew Matthew as well as Mark.

Chapter 5

Q

1. *Introduction*

'Q', the letter used for the hypothetical source that allegedly lies behind much of Matthew and Luke, sounds mysterious and intriguing. On our way through the maze, here is something that has a sense of the thrilling. To many, the term Q quickly conjures up images from *James Bond* or *Star Trek*. Perhaps, the reader thinks, this Q will be like the *James Bond* character Q, played by Desmond Llewellyn, ever able to provide some suitable new gadget appropriate to the occasion, equipping us against implausible yet dangerous situations. Or perhaps it will be like the Q of *Star Trek: The Next Generation*, an ever powerful, strangely illusive, oddly irritating presence always lurking on the sidelines to divert us from conducting our affairs in the way we would like.

Without doubt, the study of Q does carry a thrill for many scholars and students of the New Testament. Some think that this lost source provides us with a window onto the earliest years of the Christian movement, and the work of uncovering Q is now often likened to the work of excavating material in an archaeological dig. Not surprisingly, the 'discovery' in modern times of this lost document has led to something of an industry in New Testament scholarship, attempting to reconstruct its wording, its theology, its history, its origin. But before any of this is possible, there is a prior question, a question sometimes ignored, that requires careful attention; What is the evidence for this hypothetical document? How do we know that Q existed? Is the hypothesis based on solid ground or might the Q of Gospel scholarship turn out to be as fictional as the Qs of *James Bond* and *Star Trek*?

When beginning to explore the maze, we encountered two key synoptic phenomena. The first and most striking kind of material that we met was the 'Triple Tradition', material that is common to Matthew, Mark and Luke. It is this material that was our primary focus in

Chapter 3, for the standard explanation of the Triple Tradition is Markan Priority, the theory that Mark was used by both Matthew and Luke. The second kind of material we encountered was the phenomenon of 'Double Tradition', material that occurs in both Matthew and Luke but not in Mark. The standard explanation for this material is the 'Q' hypothesis, the notion that Matthew and Luke took the Double Tradition from a source now lost to us.

Markan Priority and Q are the two aspects that make up the consensus view, the Two-Source Theory (see Fig. 1, p. 20 above).

Having looked at the first facet of this theory, Markan Priority, it is now time to progress to the second, Q. As before, it is important that the readers know their guide. While I think that Markan Priority is rightly the consensus view, my view on Q attempts to challenge the consensus. It can be shown that the standard arguments for the existence of Q are flawed and that the hypothesis is simply unable to bear the weight of the evidence against it. This demonstration, though, will have to wait largely until our next chapter. Before that, it will be necessary to explain the grounds for the postulation of Q so that the reader can see clearly why it is usually regarded as necessary.

Summary

- Q is the name given to an hypothetical source commonly invoked to explain the existence of the *Double Tradition*. Mark and Q are Matthew and Luke's 'two sources', hence the term the *Two-Source Theory*.

2. *The Double Tradition*

First, we should revise our acquaintance with the Double Tradition. Double Tradition is the name given to material that is common to Matthew and Luke but which is not found in Mark. There are between 200 and 250 verses of such material and these verses are characterized by a relative lack of narrative material. These verses include the Lost Sheep, the Lord's Prayer, the Beatitudes, the Parable of the Talents (or Pounds), the Centurion's Servant (or Son), and many other well-known passages.

Double Tradition appears in the Synopsis (naturally) in two columns, one for Matthew and one for Luke. The degree of agreement in wording between Matthew and Luke varies. Sometimes there is almost a hundred per cent verbatim agreement, as with John the Baptist's preaching:

Matthew 3.7-10	*Luke 3.7-9*
'Offspring of vipers! Who warned you to flee from the coming wrath? Bear fruit therefore worthy of repentance and do not *presume* to say in yourselves, "We have Abraham as father"; for I say to you that God is able from these stones to raise up children to Abraham. Already the axe is laid at the root of the trees; for every tree not producing good fruit is cut down and cast into the fire'.	'Offspring of vipers! Who warned you to flee from the coming wrath? Bear fruit therefore worthy of repentance and do not *begin* to say in yourselves, "We have Abraham as father"; for I say to you that God is able from these stones to raise up children to Abraham. Already the axe is laid at the root of the trees; for every tree not producing good fruit is cut down and cast into the fire'.

Here, only the Greek words for 'presume' and 'begin' differ.

Though on other occasions (for example the parables of the Great Supper and the Talents/Pounds, Mt. 22.1-14//Lk. 14.16-24) the wording is not so close, the verbatim identity in passages like this indicates some sort of literary link between Matthew and Luke, a literary link in addition to their common dependence on Mark. The Double Tradition material of this kind might then be explained in any of three ways:

1.   Matthew used Luke.
2.   Luke used Matthew.
3.   Matthew and Luke both used a third document now lost to us.

Of these three options for explaining the origin of the Double Tradition material, option 3 is by far the most popular. The third document postulated is given the name Q, probably originating from the German for 'source', *Quelle*. Q is thought to be necessary for several reasons. In this chapter our main task will be to look at these reasons.

Summary

*   The *Double Tradition* is non-Markan material common to Matthew and Luke. The frequent near verbatim identity points to some kind of literary link. The usual explanation is that Matthew and Luke were both dependent on a lost source, Q.

3. *The Case for Q*

Q is a derivative hypothesis. It is the result of a prior assertion, that Matthew and Luke used Mark independently of one other. As soon as one has postulated that Matthew and Luke are independent of each other but at the same time dependent on Mark, it is the natural next step to suggest that their common non-Markan material comes from a third, otherwise unknown source. Therefore many of the traditional arguments for Q are actually—quite naturally—arguments against the dependence of one evangelist (usually Luke) on another (usually Matthew). In other words, arguments against option 2 in the list above, Luke's use of Matthew, are constituted as arguments in favour of option 3, mutual dependence on a hypothetical document. The theory that Matthew has read Luke (option 1) is rarely put forward by sensible scholars and will not be considered here.

The first four arguments below are of this type: they are arguments against Luke's use of Matthew, and so in favour of the Q hypothesis. But there are also, especially in more recent literature on the Synoptic Problem, arguments that are more positive. The fifth and sixth arguments below are like this. In other words, the first four arguments below give the same negative reason for believing in Q: that the alternative, Lukan knowledge of Matthew, is untenable. The fifth and sixth arguments below are positive: that Q is a helpful hypothesis.

Summary

- The case for Q depends largely on the prior assertion that Matthew and Luke are independent of one another. Thus arguments in favour of Q are often, in effect, arguments against the primary alternative, Luke's direct use of Matthew.

Argument 1. Luke's Order
Many argue that Luke's arrangement of Double Tradition material is inexplicable on the assumption that he has used Matthew. While a lot of the Double Tradition appears in Matthew in five nicely structured blocks of thematically related discourse (Mt. 5–7, 10, 13, 18, 24–25), the same material appears in Luke in a radically different format, much of it in a big central section (sometimes called 'The Travel Narrative',

Lk. 9.51–18.14). The point is felt so strongly that scholars have characterized Luke's treatment (on this assumption) as the work of a 'crank',
or as one who has 'demolished' his source, or who has 'unscrambled
the egg with a vengeance'. Graham Stanton, for example, says that if
Luke read Matthew, he 'has virtually demolished Matthew's carefully
constructed discourses'[1] and Christopher Tuckett asks, 'If Luke knew
Matthew, why has he changed the Matthean order so thoroughly, dis-
rupting Matthew's clear and concise arrangement of the teaching material into five blocks, each concerned with a particular theme?'[2]

An important aspect of this argument is that Matthew often seems to
find an appropriate Markan context for Double Tradition material while
Luke does so more rarely. The John the Baptist material and the Temptations, which feature both Markan and Q elements, occur in the same
context in all three Synoptics, but after this, Matthew and Luke usually
diverge in their placement of Q pericopae. Matthew and Luke differ
fairly consistently in their placing of this material.

There is one passage that is regarded as making the point with
special clarity, the Sermon on the Mount (Mt. 5–7), for if Luke used
Matthew, he cut the length of his Sermon considerably, writing the less
memorable Sermon on the Plain (Lk. 6.17-49), omitting much and
distributing the remainder at many different points in the Gospel. Fitzmyer, for example, asks, 'Why would Luke have wanted to break up
Matthew's sermons, especially the Sermon on the Mount, incorporating
only a part of it into his Sermon on the Plain and scattering the rest of it
in an unconnected form in the loose context of the travel account'.[3]

Since Matthew's Sermon is widely regarded as one of the finest
pieces of religious writing of all time, most have felt it to be unlikely
that Luke would have disturbed, rewritten and spoilt his source. It is
seen as more plausible that Matthew composed the Sermon using the
shorter discourse in Q, best represented now by Luke's Sermon on the
Plain, at the same time incorporating elements from elsewhere in Q as
well as adding fresh material.

---

1.   Graham N. Stanton, 'Matthew, Gospel of', *DBI*, pp. 432-35 (434).

2.   Christopher M. Tuckett, 'Synoptic Problem', *ABD*, VI, pp. 263-70 (268).

3.   J.A. Fitzmyer, *The Gospel According to Luke: Introduction, Translation and Notes*. I–IX (Anchor Bible, 28A, New York: Doubleday, 1981), p. 74; cf. Tuckett, 'Synoptic Problem', *ABD*, VI, p. 268.

Summary

- Luke's order of Double Tradition material, and especially his rearrangement of the Sermon on the Mount, seems inexplicable on the assumption that he used Matthew.

Argument 2. Luke's Ignorance of Matthew's Additions to Mark

Another German scholar, Werner Georg Kümmel, wrote an *Introduction to the New Testament* in the 1960s that is still widely used today. He has a short discussion of the Q hypothesis in which he asks, 'Is it conceivable that Luke would have taken over none of the Matthean additions to the Markan text?'[4] If Luke knew Matthew as well as Mark, he must have paid little attention to Matthew's versions of Mark's material. If Luke knew only Mark and Q, on the other hand, this failure to feature Matthew's additions to Mark is entirely explicable.

Mt. 12.5-7 is typical of the examples given. It is an insertion into Mk 2.23-28 par. (Cornfield), which features additional justification for the breaking of the Sabbath, including a quotation from Hos. 6.6. Or 14.28-31 is mentioned, where Peter walks on the water, in the middle of the Markan pericope in which Jesus walks on the water (Mk 6.45-52//Mt. 14.22-33). Or there is 16.17-19, in which Jesus commends Peter in the middle of the pericope of his Confession at Caesarea Philippi (Mk 8.27-30, par.):

Matthew 16.15-19	Mark 8.29-30	Luke 9.20-21
15. He said to them, 'But who do you say that I am?' 16. Simon Peter replied, 'You are the Christ, the Son of the living God'. 17. And Jesus answered him, 'Blessed are you, Simon Bar-Jona! For flesh and blood has not revealed this to you, but my Father who is in heaven. 18. And I tell you, you are	29. And he asked them, 'But who do you say that I am?' Peter answered him, 'You are the Christ'.	20. And he said to them, 'But who do you say that I am?' And Peter answered, 'The Christ of God'.

4. Kümmel, *Introduction to the New Testament*, p. 50.

Peter, and on this rock I will build my church, and the powers of death shall not prevail against it. 19. I will give you the keys of the kingdom of heaven, and whatever you bind on earth shall be bound in heaven, and whatever you loose on earth shall be loosed in heaven'. 20. Then he strictly charged the disciples to tell no one that he was the Christ.	30. And he charged them to tell no one about him.	21. But he charged and commanded them to tell this to no one…

One can see the point at a glance. There is some interesting, non-Markan material in Matthew 16.17-19 that has no parallel in Luke. The question always asked is, Why, on the assumption that Luke used Matthew as well as Mark, would he have omitted this fresh Matthaean material?

Other examples might be given, but the point seems clear. If Luke knew Matthew, it is regarded as strange that he apparently shows no knowledge of such Matthaean additions to Mark. And if Luke was ignorant of Matthew in passages like these, he was ignorant of Matthew everywhere, and so the Q hypothesis becomes necessary in order to make sense of the Double Tradition.

Summary

- Luke appears to be ignorant of Matthew's modifications of Mark. This is inexplicable on the assumption that he knew Matthew.

Argument 3. Luke's Lack of 'M' Material

As we saw when surveying the data in Chapter 2 above, there is a large body of material that occurs only in Matthew, the material that is known as 'special Matthew' or 'M'. Those who question Luke's use of Matthew point out that this material is entirely absent in Luke and thus that he must have been ignorant of his Gospel. Fitzmyer, for example, asks, 'If Luke depended on Matthew, why did he constantly omit

Matthean material in episodes lacking Markan parallels, e.g. in the infancy and resurrection narratives?'[5]

The argument sounds circular—Luke does not feature the M material, the passages found only in Matthew, by definition. But the point generally made is that it seems unlikely that Luke would have omitted so much of this rich Matthaean material. Luke's omission of the visit of the Gentile magi (Mt. 2.1-12) in Matthew's Birth Narrative, for example, is thought unlikely for an evangelist like Luke who was so interested in the Gentile mission. It is added more broadly that Luke's Birth Narrative (Lk. 1–2) is so radically different from Matthew's (Mt. 1–2) that again it is unlikely that Luke knew of it.

This argument is related to the previous one, not least given that some of Matthew's special material (M) seems to occur in Triple Tradition contexts (as we saw in Chapter 2, above). Both of these arguments focus on what is present in Matthew but lacking in Luke, just as with Markan Priority one looks at what is present in Matthew and Luke but lacking in Mark.

Summary

- Matthew's special material ('M') does not feature at all in Luke, a sign that Luke did not know Matthew's Gospel.

Argument 4. Alternating Primitivity

The argument against Luke's use of Matthew, and so in favour of the Q hypothesis, is strengthened further by a fourth consideration. If Luke read Matthew, his versions of Double Tradition material ought always to be secondary to Matthew's versions of the same material. On that theory he would, after all, always be writing after Matthew and thus with earlier versions of sayings in front of him, something that, according to most, is manifestly not the case. Rather, it seems to be the case that sometimes Matthew preserves the more original form of a saying appearing in the Double Tradition; sometimes Luke preserves the more original form. This, it is thought, would be inexplicable if one evangelist (Luke) is following the other (Matthew).

Thus, sometimes Luke seems to be secondary to Matthew, as here, for example:

5.   Fitzmyer, *Luke I–IX*, p. 75.

Matthew 7.11	Luke 11.13
'If you, then, who are evil, know how to give good gifts to your children, how much more will your Father who is in heaven give *good gifts* to those who ask him'.	'If you, then, who are evil, know how to give good gifts to your children, how much more will your Father who is in heaven give *the Holy Spirit* to those who ask him'.

Most believe that Q featured the term 'good gifts', which makes good literary sense of the material that has preceded this conclusion, which talks about 'good gifts'. Luke, with his special interest in the Holy Spirit, is then thought to have changed the Q version that is now better represented by Matthew.

Points like this, Matthaean Priority in Q material, cause no problems for the thesis of Luke's knowledge of Matthew, but the situation does not always seem to be like this. The Q theory seems to be demanded by the presence on other occasions of more primitive wording in Luke's form of Double Tradition material. Perhaps the most popular examples of supposed Lukan priority in Q material are the Lord's Prayer (Lk. 11.2-4; cf. Mt. 6.9-13), the Beatitudes (Lk. 6.20-23; cf. Mt. 5.3-12) and the doom oracle (Lk. 11.49-51; cf. Mt. 23.34-36). Luke's Lord's Prayer, to begin with, is more terse than Matthew's. It is thought unlikely that Luke would have reworked the (now more popular) Matthaean version:

Matthew 6.9-13	Luke 11.2b-4
9. *Our* Father *who art in heaven,* Hallowed be thy name	Father, Hallowed be thy name.
10. Thy kingdom come. *Thy will be done, On earth as it is in heaven.*	Thy kingdom come.
11. Give us this day our bread for the morrow;	3. Give us each day our bread for the morrow;
12. And forgive us our debts, As we also have forgiven our debtors;	4. And forgive us our sins, For we ourselves forgive every one who is indebted to us;
13. And lead us not into temptation, *But deliver us from evil.*	And lead us not into temptation.

It is thought unlikely that Luke would have abbreviated the Matthaean version that is now so familiar to us, omitting lines like 'Thy will be done, On earth as it is in heaven' and 'deliver us from evil'. The Q version of the prayer, then, will probably have looked more like Luke's version, and the extra Matthaean parts (including 'Our Father who art in heaven') will be distinctively Matthaean additions.

Likewise the Beatitudes. Luke's 'Blessed are the poor' (Lk. 6.20) is thought likely to be the original Q form from which Matthew developed his 'spiritualized' version 'Blessed are the poor in Spirit' (Mt. 5.3). The reverse direction, the notion that Luke derived his down-to-earth 'Blessed are (you) poor' from Matthew's 'Blessed are the poor in spirit' is thought to be quite unlikely.

In all these and other cases, it is felt that the Lukan version is less characteristically Lukan than the Matthean version is characteristically Matthean, a situation easily explicable if both are independently redacting an unknown source, Q, but implausible if Luke is redacting Matthew.

Summary

- Sometimes Matthew, and sometimes Luke seems to have the more primitive form of Double Tradition material. If Luke had used Matthew, one would have expected Matthew always to have the more primitive form, and Luke always to be secondary.

Argument 5. The Distinctive Character of Q

Forms of these four arguments (order; the lack of Matthaean additions to Mark in Luke; Luke's lack of M material; and alternating primitivity) have been important in the establishment of the Q hypothesis. They have been repeated many times over at least the last century or so. The four arguments work on the assumption that by demonstrating the implausibility of Luke's use of Matthew, one establishes the plausibility of the Q hypothesis.

It would be a mistake, however, to think of Q as depending solely on negative reasoning. The hypothesis is not simply about the unlikelihood of Luke's knowledge of Matthew. It is also about the probability of Q. There is, therefore, a second category of argument concerning the existence of Q and it is based on the notion that Q makes its presence felt in the Gospels. It distinguishes itself from the other material in the

Synoptics not purely because it provides a preferable explanation for the phenomenon of the Double Tradition but also because it is held to have a special theology, vocabulary, history, structure and style. Q is not the same as Matthew and it is distinct from Luke.

The importance of this argument for Q should not be underestimated. Indeed, if anything, it has grown stronger in recent years. Though sometimes spelt out explicitly, this argument is more often an implicit one. There is now a vast amount of literature studying Q as a document in its own right. Just as scholars have investigated the origins, characteristics, theology, community and genre of each of the Synoptic Gospels, so too they are now investigating Q along the same lines. The research, like similar research into the Gospels, is wide-ranging, and Q scholars argue among each other about their conclusions. But one implicit consensus emerges: that Q is a document in its own right that does not look like Matthew, Mark or Luke. Its distinctiveness is becoming an important argument in its favour.

Summary

- There are also two more positive arguments for the existence of Q, which do not focus on the implausibility of Luke's use of Matthew.
- The first of these arguments is that Q has a distinctive character. Q is very different from Matthew and from Luke. There is 'space' between the theology, history, genre and character of Q and the theology, history, genre and character of the Synoptics. Q makes its presence felt.

Argument 6. The Redaction-Critical Case

There is, further, a third category of argument, in addition to those from the unlikelihood of Lukan use of Matthew and from the distinctiveness of Q. Like the latter argument, this one has surfaced relatively recently. It depends on the success of a related discipline, *redaction-criticism*, a tool—let us remind ourselves—that might be defined as the study of the way in which an author 'redacts' (edits) his source material with a view to ascertaining the theological standpoint of the text and its author. But in order to study the ways in which an author uses his source material, one has to have an idea of what that source material is.

On the whole, scholars have worked with the assumption that Matthew and Luke were using Mark and Q. It is then thought that the success with which the redaction-critics' work has been done provides a corroboration of the starting-point, the postulation of Matthew's and Luke's independent use of (Mark and) Q. The argument is stated succinctly by Graham Stanton: 'The success of redaction criticism in clarifying the literary methods and distinctive theological emphases of Matthew and Luke on the assumption of dependence on Mark and Q is an important argument in favour of the two-source hypothesis'.[6] This argument is perhaps the consideration that is most weighty in the mind of the majority of contemporary scholars. What it amounts to is a *laissez-faire* argument in favour of a conservative position: one ought to maintain the status quo in the light of the fine scholarship that the consensus has produced. As the popular saying goes, 'If it ain't broke, don't fix it'.

Though the fifth argument, from the distinctiveness of Q, is important, this one is more important still, for many believe in Q but (relatively) few write books about it. This large, Q-believing majority, takes the hypothesis for granted in its books on the New Testament, and every time it is presupposed, the argument for Q apparently gains more ground. In other words, if Q consistently makes sense in so many different studies on the New Testament, it would seem to be a workable hypothesis. And a workable hypothesis might well seem to be a plausible hypothesis.

Summary

- Those who have assumed the Q hypothesis have produced plausible redaction-critical studies of Matthew and Luke. This is therefore a sign that the Q hypothesis is helpful and plausible.

4. *Conclusion*

There are, then, six key arguments that tend to be used in the attempt to establish the Q hypothesis. The first four of these are essentially negative arguments, arguments against Luke's use of Matthew. The other

---

6. Stanton, 'Matthew, Gospel of', p. 35.

two arguments are positive arguments that attempt to establish the usefulness of the Q hypothesis. Let us summarize:

(a)   *It is unlikely that Luke knew Matthew*: The source for the non-Markan material that they share (Double Tradition) must therefore be a third, otherwise unknown source. It is unlikely that Luke knew Matthew for the following reasons:
   - *Luke's order* is inexplicable on the assumption that he knew Matthew.
   - *Luke's ignorance of Matthew's modifications of Mark*: This too would be inexplicable on the assumption that he knew Matthew.
   - *Luke's lack of M material*: Matthew's special material ('M') does not feature at all in Luke, a sign that Luke did not know his Gospel.
   - *Alternating primitivity in the Double Tradition*: Sometimes Matthew and sometimes Luke seems to have the more primitive form of Double Tradition material. If Luke had used Matthew, one would have expected Luke always to be secondary.

(b)   *Q has a distinctive character*: Q is very different from Matthew and from Luke. There is 'space' between the theology, history, genre and character of Q and the theology, history, genre and character of the Synoptics. Q makes its presence felt.

(c)   *Q aids the task of redaction-criticism*: Scholars who have taken the Q hypothesis for granted have been successful redaction-critics of the Synoptic Gospels.

Of course, all these arguments work together in the attempt to demonstrate the plausibility of the Q hypothesis, mutually supporting and illustrating one another. It is particularly difficult, for example, to distinguish between the first two arguments above, the question of Luke's order and the question of Luke's ignorance of Matthew's modifications of Mark. Indeed they might simply be seen as two aspects of the same basic argument, an argument that might be summarized in the following way:

   - It is difficult to believe that Luke knew Matthew given his treatment of the Double Tradition material in relation to his treatment of the Triple Tradition material.

Or, to state the same thing more positively:

- The Two-Source Theory makes good sense of Luke's Gospel, explaining both the way that the Double Tradition appears in it and also the way in which the Triple Tradition appears in it.

Further, this takes for granted the argument from redaction-criticism, for redaction-criticism is, as a discipline, all about 'making good sense' of the Gospels.

How plausible, though, are these arguments? They have certainly been influential and are often repeated. Versions of at least some of these will be found in all introductions to the Synoptic Problem that argue in favour of the Two-Source Theory. What is less often found is a clear statement of the case against Q, or of an attempt to explore the above points more carefully. In the next chapter, then, we will focus on the case against Q, attempting to see whether the points above are capable of a plausible answer and, furthermore, whether the alternative case—for Luke's use of Matthew—might be more plausible still.

Before doing this, though, let us pause for a moment to consider the language in which the arguments tend to be presented—the manner is striking because the language is so strong. It seems that scholars are unable to talk about the hypothesis of Luke's use of Matthew without resorting to strings of rhetorical questions, with exclamation marks, joke quotation marks, humorous imagery and, at times, even ridicule. In most of the examples above, especially in the first four arguments, the rhetoric is forceful. There are questions that do not require answers ('Is it conceivable… ?'; 'What could have moved Luke… ?') and plenty of rhetorical flourishes ('unscrambling the egg with a vengeance'). Matters do not seem to be implausible, unlikely or improbable. Rather, they are 'untenable', 'inexplicable' and 'incomprehensible'. Likewise, Luke does not disturb or alter Matthew's arrangements—he 'destroys' or 'demolishes' them.

Why, then, is the language is so strong? Part of the answer is that it is often a function of its context. The arguments for the existence of Q tend to occur in introductory pieces, Bible dictionaries, introductions to commentaries and similar, in which the scholar has word-limits to worry about and the reader's patience at stake. Because of the limited space, rhetorical questions and overstatement stand in for patient argumentation. But this is not the whole picture.

A second reason for the inflated rhetoric is probably the conscious imitation and unconscious influence of the most marked use of such language, B.H. Streeter's famous attempt to dispose of the theory that Luke used Matthew, an attempt that dates back to a seminal volume called *The Four Gospels* published in 1924. Here Streeter wrote the following paragraph:

> If then Luke derived this material from Matthew, he must have gone through both Matthew and Mark so as to discriminate with meticulous precision between Marcan and non-Marcan material; he must then have proceeded with the utmost care to tear every little piece of non-Marcan material he desired to use from the context of Mark in which it appeared in Matthew—in spite of the fact that contexts in Matthew are always exceedingly appropriate—in order to re-insert it into a different context of Mark having no special appropriateness. A theory which would make an author capable of such a proceeding would only be tenable if, on other grounds, we had reason to believe he was a crank.[7]

This statement is often quoted and frequently echoed. Its influence has been overwhelming. This is not surprising since the wonderful rhetoric is instantly memorable. No one wants to believe that Luke is a 'crank': they neither want to slander Luke nor to risk the charge of being stupid themselves. Nor does anyone, with the slightest acquaintance with Luke's Gospel, want to feel that it could have been made up of a perverse combing, tearing up and inappropriate restructuring of Matthew. Streeter wins the day before the reader has even opened up the Synopsis. As we will go on to see, however, the rhetoric is empty: not only is the statement based on a rather dubious judgment of taste (preferring Matthew's mechanical, thematic arrangements to Luke's orderly, narrative-sensitive arrangements) but also Streeter misrepresents the facts (Luke does not, on the assumption that he is using Mark and Matthew, reinsert non-Markan Matthean material into 'a different context of Mark').

Leaving that aside for a moment, one might guess at a further reason for the excessive rhetoric. I suspect that for many there is a certain feeling of frustration that debates over the Synoptic Problem continue to rage on from year to year, that Q sceptics obstinately refuse to acknowledge the supposed triumph of the Two-Source Theory. There is the attitude that these are issues that were settled long ago—the foundations were laid successfully and scholars have been building on

---

7.   B.H. Streeter, *The Four Gospels: A Study of Origins* (London: Macmillan, 1924), p. 183.

them without trouble ever since. Not only are Q sceptics a nuisance, but they also appear to have a certain arrogance, the surprising and implausible notion that they might be able to overturn the consensus of a century.

Conversely, it is easy for Q sceptics to underestimate the sheer persuasive force that the consensus, simply by virtue of its being the consensus, continues to exert. This is particularly the case in relation to the redaction-critical argument. In book after book and article after article, reasonable sense seems to be made of Matthew and Luke on the assumption that they utilized Mark independently of one another. What are a handful of publications, however erudite, against an avalanche of books and articles making good literary, theological and historical sense of Matthew and Luke, to say nothing of Christian origins more broadly, on the assumption of Q?

It is worth seeing, though, that the rhetoric does communicate something important. While caricature and overstatement may not be the way to truth, the language used in the standard arguments for Q performs a function—it is attempting to show the student in an instant just how implausible the thesis of Luke's knowledge of Matthew is held to be. It is saying, in effect, 'Can you really believe *this*?' That is why the rhetoric is most strident when one is dealing with the negative arguments (1–4 above). There is less reason for it when calmly stating positive reasons for believing in Q.

What we will want to know is whether the extremity of this reaction against Luke's use of Matthew is justified. Is it obvious that matters like alternating primitivity or the order of Double Tradition material firmly establish Matthew's and Luke's independence from one another? Are the data described accurately by opponents of Luke's use of Matthew and Mark? If so, can Q-sceptical answers be credible? Let us take a little time to investigate these issues with a clear head and a sharp eye, leaving behind the excesses of rhetoric, and proceeding through the maze with sobriety and care.

Chapter 6

THE CASE AGAINST Q

1. *Introduction*

Let us take stock and see where we have arrived. So far, we have seen that the key to synoptic interrelationships is the consensus theory of Markan Priority. This theory, which states that Matthew and Luke both made direct use of Mark, makes better sense of the data than does its main competitor, the theory that Mark wrote third, utilizing Matthew and Luke. We have also had a look at the arguments in favour of its sister theory, the Q hypothesis. The Q hypothesis is primarily dependent on the notion that not only did Matthew and Luke use Mark but that they also used Mark *independently* of one another. As soon as one has stated this, Matthew's and Luke's independent use of Mark, the Q hypothesis is the logical corollary: a text is needed that can explain the close, verbal agreements between Matthew and Luke in passages that are not in Mark (namely 'the Double Tradition'). Most of the arguments for Q therefore tend to be arguments in favour of Matthaean and Lukan independence from one another, though—as we have seen—other kinds of argument for the existence of Q are also beginning to emerge.

Now it is my view, as I have already hinted, that each one of the standard arguments for Q is capable of refutation. Not only has the persuasiveness of the standard arguments been greatly overestimated by many scholars but the same scholars have also tended to underestimate the positive evidence in favour of Luke's use of Matthew. Let us proceed through the next part of the maze, then, following this route. First, we will look at answers to the arguments for Q that were laid out in the previous chapter, noting that not one of them is strong enough to make the case. Then we will look closely at evidence in favour of Luke's use of Matthew and will conclude by reflecting on the possibility of a world without Q. This chapter will be a little longer than previous ones because the task is larger: to look at both the problems with the standard case for Q and to make the positive case for Luke's use of Matthew.

First, though, let us remind ourselves of the shape of the theory that is defended here (see Fig. 2 above, p. 22).

Q has no part to play in the Farrer Theory, which is also known as 'the Farrer–Goulder theory', 'Mark without Q' or 'Markan Priority without Q'. The notion that Luke has direct access to the Gospel of Matthew as well as to the Gospel of Mark enables one, as Austin Farrer (the scholar responsible for the theory) put it, to 'dispense with Q'.[1] Second, one should notice that Mark remains at the top of the diagram: Markan Priority is strongly affirmed. The Farrer Theory should not be confused with the Griesbach Theory, which rejects not only Q but also Markan Priority. Reputable scholars have been known to confuse the two theories or even to be ignorant of any difference between them. Indeed it is still often assumed, especially in American scholarship, that the case against the Griesbach Theory is identical with the case in favour of the Two-Source Theory, a state of affairs that helps to supervise the dominance of the consensus position on Q. It is sometimes assumed that arguments in favour of Markan Priority themselves constitute arguments in favour of Q, a position that is quite mistaken.

Summary

- *The Farrer Theory* affirms Markan Priority but suggests that Luke also knew and used Matthew, which enables one to dispense with Q.

2. *Responding to the Arguments for Q*

Argument 1. Luke's Order

How, then, does a scholar convinced of Luke's use of Matthew respond to the point so strongly and commonly made that Luke simply *could not* have destroyed Matthew's fine ordering of material? The problem with the argument can be seen most clearly if we return to Streeter's influential formulation of it and take a careful look at it:

1.   Farrer, 'On Dispensing with Q'.

> If then Luke derived this material from Matthew, he must have gone through both Matthew and Mark so as to discriminate with meticulous precision between Marcan and non-Marcan material; he must then have proceeded with the utmost care to tear every little piece of non-Marcan material he desired to use from the context of Mark in which it appeared in Matthew—in spite of the fact that contexts in Matthew are always exceedingly appropriate—in order to re-insert it into a different context of Mark having no special appropriateness. A theory which would make an author capable of such a proceeding would only be tenable if, on other grounds, we had reason to believe he was a crank.[2]

Apart from the inflated rhetoric, there are important problems with this statement, not least that Streeter misrepresents an important fact.[3] As it stands, the statement appears convincing because the process described would indeed make Luke into something of a 'crank'. But the process is inaccurately described. Most of the pieces of Luke's Double Tradition do not appear in a 'different context of Mark', whether appropriate or otherwise, because *very little of Luke's Double Tradition occurs in a Markan context at all*. That is, whereas Matthew often features Q in Markan contexts, Luke rarely does. Most of Luke's Q material occurs in two sections, 6.20–8.3 and 9.51–18.14, and in these sections there is very little use of Mark.[4] Therefore the question we should be asking is not, Why does Luke place non-Markan material from Matthew in different Markan contexts? but rather, Why does Luke, on the whole, place non-Markan material from Matthew in non-Markan contexts?

When we frame the question accurately, the answer comes forth naturally, but in order to see it we need to notice a second major problem with Streeter's statement: it is based on a rather dubious value judgment, one that prefers Matthew's order and arrangement to Luke's. It is a judgment that we are not required to share. For while there is no doubt that Luke's ordering of the Double Tradition material is often strikingly different from Matthew's, one should not think of difference

---

2.   Streeter, *The Four Gospels*, p. 183.

3.   For the following, cf. Goulder, *Luke*, p. 39, and E.P. Sanders and M. Davies, *Studying the Synoptic Gospels* (London: SCM Press; Valley Forge, PA: Trinity Press International, 1989), pp. 114-15: Streeter's argument 'depends on one value judgment and some incorrect generalisations' (p. 114).

4.   The only exceptions to this general rule are the John the Baptist—Temptations material in Lk. 3–4 and the Parable of the Pounds in Lk. 19.11-27, the former incidents in the same Markan context and the latter a different one (from Matthew).

from Matthew as inferiority to Matthew. After all, 'Matthew's order' is precisely that, *Matthew's* order and if one pauses to think about it, it is easy to see why Luke might have wanted to alter it. Matthew's re-ordering of Mark has a particular, distinctive structure: there are five great edifices in chs 5–7 (Sermon on the Mount), 10 (Mission Discourse), 13 (Parables), 18 (Church instructions) and 24–25 (Eschatological Discourses), each a large block of Jesus' sayings, each one marked off with 'When Jesus had finished these sayings [etc.]...'. Material from Mark occurs to varying degrees in each of these structures. For example, Matthew 13 is clearly based on the shorter parable chapter in Mark 4, and Matthew 24–25 is clearly based on the shorter eschatological discourse in Mark 13. Other material from Mark is interspersed between each of these discourses. Now, what we need to ask is whether it is plausible that Luke, having come across this major restructuring of Mark by Matthew, would feel himself obliged to follow it. The answer is that Luke is highly unlikely to have wanted to follow this more rigid arrangement that we find in Matthew, in which one cannot help thinking that the narrative flow is severely and frequently compromised. From what we know of Luke's literary sensitivity and artistic ability, we are bound to conclude that Luke would not have found Matthew's restructuring of Mark congenial.

The point is reinforced in several ways. First, we can already see from Luke's use of Mark that he has a certain reticence over lengthy discourses, a reticence that suggests that he will have been more concerned still about the excessively lengthy Matthaean discourses like the Sermon on the Mount. For while Mark's Gospel does not contain anything as long as the Sermon on the Mount, there are some fairly sizeable discourses, one of which is the Parable chapter, Mark 4. Where Matthew, typically, increases the length of the chapter from Mark's 34 verses to his 52 verses (Mt. 13.1–52), Luke, equally typically, shortens it, so that his discourse is less than half the length of Mark's, only 15 verses. Mark's discourse consists of the Sower (4.1-9), its interpretation (4.13-20), the Purpose of Parables (4.10-12), the Lamp under a Bushel (4.21-25), the Seed Growing Secretly (4.26-29), the Mustard Seed (4.30-32) and a summary (4.33-34). Matthew 13 contains all this and much more. Luke, on the other hand, treats it in just the same way that, on the Farrer Theory, he treats the Sermon on the Mount. Some of it is retained, the Sower and its Interpretation (Lk. 8.4-8, 11-15), the Purpose of Parables (8.9-10) and the Lamp (8.16-18); some of it is omitted, the Seed Growing Secretly and the summary; and some of it is redistributed, the Mustard Seed (Lk. 13.18-19). Let us have a look at this in summary format:

Mark	Luke
4.1-9: Parable of the Sower	*Paralleled in 8.4-8*
4.10-12: Purpose of Parables	*Paralleled in 8.9-10*
4.13-20: Interpretation of the Sower	*Paralleled in 8.11-15*
4.21-25: Lamp Under a Bushel	*Paralleled in 8.16-18*
4.26-29: Seed Growing Secretly	*Omitted*
4.30-32: Mustard Seed	*Redistributed*: 13.18-19
4.33-34: Summary	*Omitted in Luke*

Nor is this an isolated example—the same feature is observable again with Luke's treatment of the discourse in Mk 9.33-50, Luke's parallel to which is only five verses long (Lk. 9.46-50). The point, then, is this: given Luke's clearly observable reticence over retaining long discourses in his acknowledged source Mark, it is scarcely a major leap of imagination to see the same reticence at work in his treatment of his alleged source Matthew. On the Farrer Theory, Luke here treats Matthew in the same way that we can see him treating Mark: retaining some of the substance of the discourse and omitting and redistributing the rest.[5]

Second, literary critics have now been making good sense of the order and literary design of Luke for some time. As appreciation for Luke's literary ability and for the narrative coherence of his Gospel intensifies, so too it will seem less necessary to appeal to the Q theory to explain the quirks of his order. As we saw above, Streeter's statement implies a negative value judgment on Luke's order in comparison with Matthew's, a judgment that is becoming increasingly difficult to sustain in the light of contemporary narrative-critical studies of Luke. To take just one good example, Luke places the Double Tradition pericope 'Care and Anxiety' (Mt. 6.25-34//Lk. 12.22-34), in an excellent and appropriate literary context following on from his unique parable of the Rich Fool (Lk. 12.15-21), the parable warning those members of the crowd (who still have possessions, 12.13-14) that life does not

5.   This point is developed from Goulder, *Luke*, pp. 39-41. For an answer from the perspective of the Q theory, see Christopher Tuckett, *Q and the History of Early Christianity* (Edinburgh: T. & T. Clark, 1996), pp. 26-27.

consist of the abundance of possessions, and the latter exhorting 'the disciples' (12.22) not to be anxious about their lack of possessions, something that is a prerequisite for discipleship in Luke (e.g. 5.11; 5.28; 14.33). This kind of sensitive narrative arrangement, so typical of Luke, gives some indication of how overstated it is to speak of Luke 'demolishing' Matthew's Sermon on the Mount and 'scattering the ruins to the four winds'.

Third, the idea that Luke is conservatively following the order of Q has always had difficulty with one of the most important pieces of evidence, the Lukan Preface, which seems to emphasize so strongly the matter of order. He appears to be critical of predecessors' attempts to write narratives of the Jesus story (Lk. 1.1) and he goes on to say that he has investigated everything carefully (1.2) so that he might write to Theophilus accurately and *in order* (1.3). On the Q theory, there is little reason for this overt stress on order, since Luke's order is usually taken to replicate the orders of material in his two main sources, Mark and Q order and Q's order. But on the Farrer Theory, the stress is understandable: Luke is making clear that he is critical of his predecessors' work and that his radical reordering of Matthew is in Theophilus's best interests.

Fourth, and finally, if Markan Priority is correct, it is likely that Luke has known Mark for longer than he has known Matthew. Let us say that the standard dating for Mark, somewhere in the late sixties, is correct (see above) and that the standard dating for Matthew, around 80, is also correct. Under these circumstances, Luke may well have been familiar with Mark's Gospel for some years longer than he has been acquainted with Matthew. Perhaps, let us speculate, Matthew provided the direct catalyst for Luke's reworking of Mark. He sees what Matthew has done: he has reworked Mark by adding birth and infancy narratives at one end of the Gospel, a resurrection story at the other end and adding lots of sayings material in the middle. Perhaps, Luke thinks, *he can do the same kind of thing, but do it better*, retaining Mark's essential narrative outline but expanding it by adding birth and infancy narratives at one end of the Gospel and resurrection stories at the other, adding extra material—especially sayings—in between. Indeed, not only can he use Matthew's basic idea of 'fixing' Mark in this way but he can also utilize some of this fine new Matthaean material in his own restructuring of Mark. In other words, it is easy to imagine an historical scenario that might give birth to a Gospel in which an evangelist essentially follows Mark but is at the same time influenced by and critical of Mark's first corrector. But if this kind of scenario is on the right lines, we run straight into one of the major arguments in favour of Luke's independence from Matthew, the question of Luke's alleged lack of Matthew's additions to Mark, to which we turn next.

Summary

- *Luke's order*: It is said that Luke's order of Double Tradition material is inexplicable on the assumption that he has taken it from Matthew. There are several difficulties with this argument:
  - *Dubious value judgments*: The standard argument assumes that Matthew's arrangement of Double Tradition, with its lengthy discourses, is preferable to Luke's with its emphasis on narrative movement.
  - *Comparison with Luke's use of Mark*: Luke treats Matthew's lengthy discourses in the same way that he treats Mark's discourses: he keeps some, omits some and redistributes the rest.
  - *Narrative-Criticism of Luke*: This helps us to dispense with the idea that Matthew's arrangements are superior to Luke's—Luke's rearrangements make excellent narrative-critical sense.
  - *Luke's preface* (1.1-4): This implies a critical attitude to his predecessors' order, which makes good sense on the assumption that Luke is working with Matthew as well as Mark, but less sense on the Q theory, on which Luke largely keeps Q's order.
  - *Markan Priority*: If Luke has known Mark for longer than he has known Matthew, this may well have encouraged him to prioritize its order over Matthew's.

Argument 2. Luke's Ignorance of Matthew's Additions to Mark
Let us proceed to the second major argument for Q and see whether it fairs better than the previous one. It will be useful to look at an important recent statement of the argument. This is how it is put by one of Q's most formidable defenders, Christopher Tuckett:

Luke never appears to know any of Matthew's additions to Mark in Markan material. Sometimes, in using Mark, Matthew makes substantial additions to Mark, cf. Mt. 12.5-7; 14.28-31; 16.16-19; 27.19, 24. If Luke knew Matthew, why does he never show any knowledge of Matthew's redaction of Mark? It seems easier to presume that Luke did not know any of these Matthaean additions to Mark and hence that he did not know Matthew.[6]

There are two things wrong with this argument. First, the examples given are not strong enough to make the case. Mt. 14.28-31 (listed by Tuckett second above), for example, is a Matthaean addition in the middle of the story of the Walking on the Water (Mk 6.45-52//Mt. 14.22-33), a story that is wholly absent from Luke, in either its Markan or Matthaean form. One can hardly be surprised that Luke lacks the Matthaean additions to a story that does not feature at all in his Gospel. The other examples mentioned have such a characteristically Matthaean stamp that it is straightforward to imagine why Luke might prefer the Markan version that had been more familiar to him over a longer period of time. In particular, we should not be surprised to see a Lukan version of the confession at Caesarea Philippi that does not feature that material about the ascendancy of Peter (to see the passage in synopsis, see above, pp. 111-12). After all, Luke's Gospel is not as positive about Peter overall as is Matthew's, and the narrative development of Luke–Acts—in which Peter progressively recedes further and further into the background—would seem to exclude the possibility of Luke's inclusion of the Matthaean statement. It's exactly the kind of Matthaean addition to Mark that we would expect Luke to omit.

The second problem with the argument is that it is based on a fallacy. Why does Luke not feature any of Matthew's modifications of Mark? Well, he does! On the assumption that he knows Matthew as well as Mark, Luke prefers Matthew's version to Mark's in several Triple Tradition incidents: the whole John the Baptist complex (Mt. 3; Mk 1; Lk. 3); the Temptation (Mt. 4.1-11//Mk 1.12-13//Lk. 4.1-13), the Beel-zebub Controversy (Mt. 12.22-30//Mk 3.20-27//Lk. 11.14-23) and the Mustard Seed (Mt. 13.18-19//Mk 4.30-32//Lk. 13.18-19) among them. On all of these occasions, the parallels between Matthew and Luke are more extensive than those between Mark and Luke. Indeed the early parts of each Gospel are particularly rich in examples of Luke apparently following Matthew's modified versions of the shorter Markan

6. Tuckett, *Q*, pp. 7-8.

pericope. Take John the Baptist's prophecy about Jesus, for example, which appears in all three Synoptics:

Matthew 3.11-12	Mark 1.7-8	Luke 3.16-17
11. '"I, *on the one hand*, baptize you in water for repentance, *but* the one who is coming after me is stronger than me, the shoes of whom I am not worthy to untie.	7. 'And he preached, saying, "The one who is stronger than me comes after me, the thong of whose sandals I am not worthy, having stooped down, to loose. 8. I baptized you in water [cf. Mt. 3.11//Lk. 3.16], but he will baptize you in holy spirit".'	16. 'And John answered, saying to all, "I, *on the one hand*, baptize you in water *but* the one who is stronger than me comes after me, the thong of whose sandals I am not worthy to loose.
He will baptize you in holy spirit *and fire*. 12. *His winnowing fork is in his hand and he will clear his threshing floor and he will gather his wheat into his granary, but the chaff he will burn with unquenchable fire*".'		He will baptize you in holy spirit *and fire*. 17. *His winnowing fork is in his hand to clear his threshing floor and to gather the wheat into his granary, but the chaff he will burn with unquenchable fire*".'

The words in italics are particularly noteworthy in that they seem clearly to represent substantial addition to Mark by Matthew, material then paralleled in Luke, quite clearly refuting the claim that such material 'never' occurs. The same is true in the nearby story of the Temptation of Jesus. Mark's version (Mk 1.12-13) is only two verses long, whereas Matthew (Mt. 4.1-11) and Luke (Lk. 4.1-13) both have an extended story featuring a major dialogue between Jesus and the Satan with the three famous temptations and rebuttals. Once again, it will seem to the scholar assuming Markan Priority without Q that the simple Markan story has been elaborated by Matthew and copied by Luke. Or, to put it another way, Luke has here preferred to use Matthew's substantial modification of the Markan story. The argument from Luke's lack of Matthew's modifications of Mark seems to be refuted by a simple glance at the Synopsis.

Why then is the argument still made? Surely Q theorists know about such features? Indeed they do, but their force tends not to be felt for two reasons. First, some of the most impressive examples of this feature come, as we have seen, in Luke 3–4, covering material like John the Baptist and the Temptations. This is usually admitted as a major exception to the rule, an exception that is not then allowed to cause doubt about the basic proposition. Second, the difficulty for the Q theory tends not to be spotted because examples of this kind are placed in a special category described as 'Mark–Q overlap'. 'Mark–Q overlap' passages might be more neutrally described as passages occurring in all three Synoptics in which Mark is not clearly the middle term, or, to put it another way, as the category of passages that blur the usually more straightforward distinction between 'Triple Tradition' and 'Double Tradition' (see further Chapter 2). The sharp reader will be quick to see the fallacy at the base of this argument for Q. For where Luke (on the assumption of Markan Priority without Q) prefers the Matthaean version of a pericope shared with Mark, this automatically goes into the 'Mark–Q overlap' category. And where Luke prefers the Markan version of a pericope shared with Matthew, this is held to demonstrate his lack of knowledge of the Matthaean versions of Markan pericopae. This argument is particularly weak and it should be dropped from future defences of the Q theory.

Summary

- The argument from *Luke's ignorance of Matthew's additions to Mark* runs into insurmountable problems:
- *The examples given are weak*: Luke's omissions are quite natural when one looks at them in line with his redactional interests.
- *The argument is based on a fallacy*: wherever Luke features Matthew's additions to Mark, these are placed in the category 'Mark–Q overlap' and, as far as this argument is concerned, they are ignored.

Argument 3. Luke's Lack of M Material

In some ways, the third argument for the existence of Q, Luke's lack of Matthew's Special Material ('M') is weaker still. There is an obvious circularity in this argument: of course Luke does not include 'M' material. Any substantive material he included from Matthew would automatically have become, to use the Two-Source Theory's nomenclature, 'Q' material. Or, to put it another way, any of Matthew's Special Material used by Luke would cease to be Matthew's Special Material and would become instead Double Tradition. This objection is largely conceded by Q theorists, but they add that Luke's Birth Narrative is so radically different from Matthew's that it is unlikely he knew of it; and they claim in addition that Luke would not have rejected the very rich material that M constitutes.

Several important points need to be made here. First, one has to note that knowledge of a source is not the same as direct use of a source, and the important question is whether there are any signs of Luke's knowledge of Matthew in the Birth Narrative. He may well, after all, have been inspired and informed by it without necessarily utilizing it in any extensive way. Now there are indeed some signs that Luke knows Matthew's Birth Narrative. Not only do they agree on matters unique to the two of them within the New Testament, like Jesus' birth in Bethlehem, the name of Jesus' father (Joseph) and, most importantly, the Virginal Conception, but they even share words in common, including this key sentence: [7]

Matthew 1.21	*Luke 1.31*
She *will give birth to a son and you shall call him Jesus.*	You *will give birth to a son and you shall call him Jesus*

Perhaps Matthew's Birth Narrative gave Luke the idea of writing a Birth Narrative of his own. Because of our familiarity with the Birth Narratives, we assume that prefacing a Gospel with a Birth Narrative is a self-evidently obvious thing to do, but neither Mark nor John thought that it was such an obvious thing to do, and, all things considered, the presence of a Birth Narrative in Luke is probably a sign that Luke knows Matthew. Moreover, if, as seems likely, Luke thought that he could improve on Matthew's account, then subsequent history, devotion and liturgy have agreed with him. It is from Luke that we get our shepherds, our choir of angels and our manger; it is from Luke that we

---

7.   I am grateful to Jeff Peterson for this point. The phrase is identical in the Greek. Note how in both cases it is a singular verb, 'You (sg.) shall name him Jesus.' This is addressed to Joseph in Matthew, who then indeed 'named him Jesus' (1.25), but not so appropriately to Mary in Luke, who is not going to be solely responsible for naming him (cf. 1.59-66; 2.21).

derive our picture of Mary; and it is from Luke that we take our canticles, the Benedictus, the Magnificat and the Nunc Dimittis.[8]

If this explains the differing Birth Narratives, what of the rest of Matthew? Why did Luke omit so much of it? If one has a look again at the 'M' material (see above, Chapter 2), one cannot help noticing that it is largely defined by very particularly Matthaean interests. In other words, this is like the question raised in the previous section. One will expect Luke to include only the 'Luke-pleasing' elements from Matthew, and the more one looks at the M material, the more one notices just how little it fits with Luke's literary and theological interests. We will return to this issue below. For the time being, let us note that this argument for the existence of Q is an unpersuasive one.

Summary

- Luke lacks Matthew's Special Material by definition. Where Matthew's non-Markan material appears in Luke, it is called 'Double Tradition'.
- Although he does not utilize it extensively, there are signs that Luke knows Matthew's Birth Narrative.
- The 'M' material all looks like 'Luke-displeasing' material, just what we would expect on the Farrer Theory.

Argument 4. Alternating Primitivity

The argument that works from the allegation that sometimes Matthew, sometimes Luke has the more original form of Q sayings is perhaps the most influential of the arguments in favour of Q. It is certainly one of the arguments most regularly cited by those attempting to establish Q. However, careful analysis of the argument shows that there are weaknesses in using it as if the data under discussion inevitably point to the existence of Q. The data are at least equally well explained on the assumption of the Farrer Theory. Since this does not tend to be seen in the literature, I will attempt to explain why by taking it in four steps.

---

8. The point about Luke's not including the Magi is particularly unconvincing. Yes indeed, these are Gentiles, and yes, Luke is interested in the Gentile mission, but we need to consider the whole spectrum of Luke's interests and avoid looking at only one of them. Luke is highly suspicious of magi, as we know from one of the chief villains in Acts, Simon Magus (Acts 8.9-24).

1. *Where Luke Is Agreed to Be Secondary.* There is no problem for the Farrer Theory in occasions where the Matthaean wording of a Q saying is thought to be more original than the Lukan wording, as in our example above (p. 114), where Matthew's 'good gifts' (Mt. 7.11) is almost universally regarded as more original than Luke's 'Holy Spirit' (Lk. 11.13). Here, the verdict of scholarship will be congenial to the thesis of Luke's use of Matthew.

2. *The Question of Matthaean Language.* When scholars say that Luke's versions of Q sayings are prior to Matthew's versions of those same Q sayings, they are often basing their decision on the presence of 'Matthaean language' in the Matthaean versions of the Q sayings. Where Matthew's versions feature language characteristic of Matthew, it is assumed that Matthew has added this wording to a Q saying that lacked it. Where Luke's versions lack this Matthaean wording, it is claimed that his versions are the more original ones. Such logic only works, however, once the Q hypothesis has been assumed. For if Luke used Matthew, one will expect to see Luke rewording the Matthaean original and, in the process, eliminating some of that Matthaean language. After all, one of the things that (on the Farrer Theory) will make such language distinctive of Matthew is the omission of such language by Luke. Luke's omission of the Matthaean language ultimately has the effect of making the Lukan version look more 'original'.[9]

As usual, the point is best made by means of an illustration. The following beatitude is thought to have been in Q because it is present in both Matthew and Luke:

Matthew 5.6	Luke 6.21
Blessed are those who hunger *and thirst for righteousness*, for they shall be satisfied.	Blessed are those who hunger now, for you shall be satisfied.

---

9.   This is an element in a broader phenomenon labelled the 'Matthean vocabulary fallacy' by Michael Goulder. See Goulder, *Luke*, pp. 11-15; but modified in Mark Goodacre, *Goulder and the Gospels: The Examination of a New Paradigm* (JSNTSup, 133; Sheffield: Sheffield Academic Press, 1996), pp. 83-85. For a related issue, see Michael Goulder, 'Self Contradiction in the IQP', *JBL* 118 (1999), pp. 506-17.

Many scholars have correctly pointed out that 'righteousness' is a characteristically Matthaean word. It has figures of 7/0/1, which means that it occurs seven times in Matthew, never in Mark and only once in Luke (Mt. 3.15; 5.6; 5.10; 5.20; 6.1; 6.33; 21.32; Lk. 1.75). Indeed the theme of seeking righteousness appears to be a major theme in Matthew's Gospel (see, for example, Mt. 6.33). Q theorists then infer that Luke better represents the original Q version of the saying, which Matthew has 'glossed' with one of his favourite themes. This, then, is held to be one of the occasions on which Luke's version of Q material is more 'primitive' than Matthew's version, and so closer to Q.

But the inference that Matthew is glossing a Q text better represented in Luke's version is not the only possible inference. It is just as possible, and arguably more plausible, to see Luke following Matthew and omitting his reference to 'righteousness', not least given the fact that one of the very things that will make a word specifically characteristic of Matthew is omission of that word by Luke. Under such circumstances, what we have to ask is whether the Lukan version of a given saying appears to be in line with Luke's observed practices elsewhere. And here, in Lk. 6.21, we could hardly want for a more Lukan theme than a blessing on those who 'hunger now'. This blessing is paired with a 'Woe on those who are already filled, for you will be hungry' (Lk. 6.25). Not only is the theme of 'eschatological reversal' in general one of Luke's favourites (see further on this below), but also he seems fond of the specific application to 'the hungry' being 'satisfied' and 'those already filled' getting nothing. The theme is at the heart of one of Luke's most famous and distinctive parables, the Rich Man ('who feasted sumptuously every day', Lk. 16.20) and Lazarus ('who longed to satisfy his hunger with what fell from the rich man's table', Lk. 16.21), but also it is there right at the beginning of the Gospel, in one of the key, characteristic Lukan passages, the Magnificat:

> 1.53: 'He has filled the hungry with good things and sent the rich away
> empty.'

There is little difficulty, then, in seeing Lk. 6.21 as being derived from Mt. 5.6. Luke rewrites the beatitude by eliminating the characteristically Matthaean stress on 'righteousness', instead stressing one of his own favourite themes of eschatological reversal, the hungry filled, the rich sent away empty. It is often similarly the case elsewhere that presence of characteristically Matthaean language in Matthew's versions of Q material causes people to overestimate the evidence in favour of the Q theory.

One might also draw attention to a related feature. The calculation that Lukan forms of Q sayings are sometimes more original than their Matthaean counterparts is also based on a feature of Luke's style. Luke is a subtle and versatile writer with a large vocabulary and a tendency to vary his synonyms. Matthew, on the other hand, has a more pronounced, easily recognizable style, and he does not have so rich a vocabulary. It is consequently much less straightforward to judge Lukan redactional activity than it is to pick out where Matthew has edited sources, and it is correspondingly easy to jump to the conclusion that an apparently 'un-Lukan' form is a 'pre-Lukan', Q form. Frequently one sees claims that a given word is 'un-Lukan and therefore pre-Lukan'.[10]

The appearance of more original Lukan forms in Q material is partly a consequence, therefore, of the way in which Q theorists calculate these supposedly more primitive versions. They do not pay due attention to the fact that Luke's style is so much more difficult to pin down than is Matthew's, and they do not consider the fact that the Matthaean language present in Matthew's versions might equally well tell in favour of the Farrer Theory.

3. *Neglected Arguments for Lukan Secondariness.* Regularly, arguments in favour of Lukan secondariness are simply overlooked by Q theorists. A classic example of this is the first beatitude. Let us have a look at it in synopsis:

Matthew 5.1b-3	*Luke 6.20*
'His disciples came to him, and he opened his mouth and taught them, saying:	'Looking at his disciples, he said:
"Blessed are the poor *in spirit*, for theirs is the kingdom of heaven".'	"Blessed are the poor, for yours is the kingdom of God".'

It is almost universally held that Matthew's 'in spirit' here is a secondary, 'spiritualizing' gloss on the more primitive Q version best represented by Luke. Indeed, it is a text book example of the very argument we are currently considering. But the standard view actually has,

---

10. This matter is dubbed 'the Lukan priority fallacy' by Goulder, *Luke*, pp. 15-17.

to say the least, no more going for it than does the alternative view that Luke's version is secondary, simplifying and 'secularizing' his source in Matthew. There are at least four reasons to find it plausible that Luke removed 'in spirit' from his version of the beatitude:

1. Luke's is commonly regarded as the Gospel of the poor, the destitute, the outcast, the widow, the underdog. It would be entirely in character for Luke to revise his source in the way proposed.

2. This beatitude stands at the agenda-setting outset of Jesus' second major discourse in Luke. The first major discourse, in the synagogue at Nazara (4.16-30), also begins with a blessing ('good news') on 'the poor' (4.18), where Jesus announces himself to be the one anointed to fulfil the prophecy of Isaiah 61.

3. Unlike Matthew, the beatitude in Luke has a corresponding 'woe' on 'the rich' (Lk. 6.24). This kind of thing is classic Luke and is usually given the name 'eschatological reversal', which means that the roles in the present world order are reversed in the kingdom of God. As we saw above, it has a particularly famous statement in the Magnificat (Lk. 1.46-55), and it is given special treatment in the parable of 'the rich man' and 'the poor man' (Lazarus) in Lk. 16.19-31, which one might almost regard as a narrative version of this (and the next) beatitude.

4. The narrative-critic will be sensitive to both the audience and the narrative context of this beatitude in Luke. It is spoken to 'disciples', who, in Luke, have 'left everything' (Lk. 5.11, 28) to follow Jesus. Since in Luke poverty appears to be a prerequisite for discipleship, we will hardly be surprised to see the disciples blessed as 'the poor'. Indeed we hear in 14.33, that 'None of you can become my disciple if you do not give up all your possessions' (cf. also pp. 126-27 above).

In short, a pause to consider Luke's characteristic procedure confirms that we should not be at all surprised with a change from Matthew's 'poor in spirit', a phrase, incidentally, that is found nowhere else in Matthew, to 'the poor', as distinctive a Lukan interest as one can find. This is one example among many of the existence of good arguments for Lukan secondariness in a passage where his primitivity is usually taken for granted.

4. *The Living Stream of Oral Tradition.* The issue is further complicated by the likelihood that on occasions Luke may well have preserved elements from different versions of Jesus' sayings in his oral tradition. When we were looking at Matthew's and Luke's relation to Mark, we noted the absurdity of assuming that oral traditions of the Jesus story died out as soon as the evangelists committed them to papyrus and, consequently, the likelihood that the later evangelists redacted Mark in the light of their knowledge of such oral traditions. This means that on occasion, Matthew and Luke inevitably bear witness to different, sometimes more original versions of Jesus material than the versions found in their literary source, Mark. Consequently, it is scarcely a major leap of the imagination to see Luke occasionally bearing witness to different or more original versions of sayings found in his literary source, Matthew.

Some Q sceptics feel a little uncomfortable with this scenario since it might at first sight appear to allow Q to creep in through the back door. Is this, to use another image, a kind of 'closet Q', believing in a form of the Q hypothesis but not owning up to it? I don't think so. I would prefer to call it Luke's creative, critical interaction with Mark and Matthew in the light of the living stream of oral tradition. Let us be clear: the notion that Luke was influenced by oral traditions of Jesus materials in no way compromises the theory of his literary dependence on Mark and Matthew. Unless we also believe that Matthaean versions of Triple Tradition pericopae are always and inevitably secondary to their Markan parallels, we should not find the thesis of occasional Lukan Priority in Double Tradition materials strange. Just as Matthew and Luke interacted with Mark in the light of their knowledge of similar stories from oral tradition, so too I propose that Luke interacted with Matthew in the light of his knowledge of similar material in oral tradition.

The example we used above (pp. 95-96) to see this phenomenon at work in Luke's use of Mark was the words at the institution of the Eucharist. One of the values of this example was that it was concerned with words used in early Christian liturgy, precisely the kind of place where one would expect to see this kind of thing happening, influence on Luke from oral traditions of the material he also knew from Mark.

Now one of the clearest examples given of the Lukan version of Double Tradition being prior is a similar example, the Lord's Prayer, again the kind of material that we will expect to have been subject to variation in oral tradition. Even today, where the Lord's Prayer is often known primarily orally and not in dependence on a written text, one finds local variation. The same kind of thing seems highly likely to have been the case when Luke comes to write his version of the prayer in 11.2-4. He looks at the Matthaean version but re-writes it in line with the version more familiar to him from frequent recitation in his own tradition. Just as many Catholics today end the prayer where Matthew ends it, at 'Deliver us from evil', not adding 'Thine be the kingdom, the glory and the power, for ever and ever Amen' (which is a scribal addition to Matthew, perhaps also influenced by oral tradition), so Luke ends his prayer with 'Lead us not into temptation' and not with 'But deliver us from evil', in spite of the fact that the latter is present in his text of Matthew. Just as Catholics today know of the existence of the 'Thine be the kingdom...' clause, but choose not to use it because of familiarity and loyalty to their own tradition, so too it is hardly difficult to think of Luke knowing the clause 'But deliver us from evil' but not using it for the same kind of reason.

The observation that both Matthew and Luke sometimes appear to have the more original forms of the Double Tradition material does not, then, serve to establish the existence of Q. Not only has the extent of Luke's supposed primitivity been greatly overestimated, based partly on misconstrued assessments of the presence of Matthaean language, but even on the occasions where Luke does show possible signs of primitivity, this is only evidence for Q if one is prepared to deny a role to the living stream of oral tradition in the composition of Luke's Gospel.

Summary

- *The Argument from alternating primitivity* can be countered in the following steps:
    - There are many places where all agree that *Luke is secondary*.

- *Matthaean language*: The presence of Matthew's favourite expressions in Q material is regularly taken to indicate that his versions are later than Luke's versions. But the same evidence is congenial to the thesis that Luke is using Matthew: Matthew composes the non-Markan material using characteristic expressions and Luke sometimes eliminates such expressions. Further, Luke has a much larger vocabulary than Matthew and he uses many more unusual expressions. It is a fallacy to assume that 'un-Lukan' expressions are necessarily 'pre-Lukan' expressions.

- *Neglected arguments for Lukan secondariness*: Sometimes scholars have greatly underestimated the arguments for Luke's redaction of Matthew (e.g. the Beatitudes).

- *The living stream of oral tradition*: Oral traditions did not die a death as soon as the evangelists set pen to papyrus. Just as Matthew creatively interacted with Mark in the light of oral traditions, so too did Luke with Matthew and Mark.

Argument 5. The Distinctiveness of Q

The idea that Q is distinctive, that it makes its presence felt by means of its content, genre and theology, is becoming one of the major arguments in favour of its existence. Indeed the reconstruction of Q, the analyses of its text, the studies of its supposed literary history, are all now making a major contribution to the study of the Synoptic Problem and one ignores them at one's peril. It is generally thought that it would be impossible for such convincing studies of Q as a text in its own right to be written if Q never actually existed.

It is difficult to answer this argument succinctly. Providing a carefully documented response to the many studies of Q currently circulating would require something of a major monograph itself. Nevertheless, the reader will be wise to bear in mind the following points:

(a) Studies that assume Q inevitably cause a re-entrenchment of the notion that Q is distinctive. The repeated analysis of the Double Tradition material in isolation from its Matthaean and

Lukan contexts generates a momentum of its own, the tendency of which is to reinforce the starting point, which was the isolation of the Double Tradition material from its contexts in Matthew and Luke. It is rare to see Q scholars pausing to reflect on how the same evidence appears on a Q sceptical theory, and ultimately this is the kind of thing that is needed in order to test claims that the distinctiveness of the Q material implies the existence of a Q document.

(b)   Claims about the distinctiveness of Q tend to underestimate the degree of overlap that exists between the Double Tradition (Q) and special Matthew (M). It is impossible, for example, to distinguish between the style of some of the units of M material and some of the units of Q.

(c)   It is sometimes said that Luke must have taken over some pericopae from Q that Matthew did not also take over. In other words, the hypothetical document Q overlaps with but is not identical with the Double Tradition material. It is a notorious difficulty, however, to isolate alleged Q pericopae in Luke outside of the Double Tradition, something that is odd given the claims about the distinctiveness of Q's thought and style. Indeed the candidates most commonly suggested, like Lk. 11.27-28 (Woman in the Crowd), Lk. 12.15-21 (Parable of the Rich Fool) or Lk. 15.8.10 (Lost Coin) all have an uncannily Lukan ring about them—their Lukan style is, if anything, as marked here as anywhere.

(d)   We need to bear in mind that the Double Tradition does have a distinctive profile on the Farrer Theory as well as on the Q theory. For if one assumes the Farrer Theory, Q is constituted by those parts of Matthew's non-Markan material that most appealed to Luke. Or, to put it another way, they are the 'Luke-pleasing' elements in Matthew's extra material. If one wanted to put this into an equation, it would look like this:

$$Q = \text{(Matthew minus Mark) divided by 'Luke-pleasingness'}$$

And this is something that we can test, for if Q is indeed the result of the selections from Matthew's non-Markan material that Luke found 'pleasing', then we will expect the material he left behind to be in some way Luke-displeasing. Now the material that, on the Farrer Theory,

Luke left behind is the M material or 'Special Matthew', the pericopae that are in Matthew alone. So does the Q material generally have a 'Luke-pleasing' profile and the M material a 'Luke-displeasing' profile? Indeed they do. The Q pericopae are precisely the ones we would expect Luke to take over from a book like Matthew, Jesus' ethical teaching in the Sermon on the Mount, the Centurion's Boy, the Lost Sheep, teachings about discipleship and the rest, and there is not a pericope in M that looks congenial to Luke: several have an oddly 'legendary' character (e.g. Mt. 17.24-27, Coin in the Fish's Mouth) and others are in direct conflict with Luke's theology (e.g. Mt. 25.31-46, the Sheep and the Goats). Indeed it has long been recognized that the Q material has something of a pro-Gentile profile whereas the M material tends to be inspired by and focused on the Jewish-Christian mission and interests. In other words, the general profiles of Q and M turn out to be precisely what we would expect them to be if the Farrer Theory is correct.

Summary

- *The argument from distinctiveness of Q* is not decisive:
  - The isolation of the Double Tradition from its context in Matthew and Luke inevitably generates a distinctive profile for Q.
  - The overlap between Q material and M material partly undermines the claim.
  - It is difficult to discover good candidates for material that might have derived from Q among Luke's special material.
  - The Double Tradition has a distinctive profile on the Farrer Theory, namely: (Matthew *minus* Mark) *divided by* 'Luke-pleasingness'.

Argument 6. The Success of Redaction-Criticism
Redaction-criticism of Matthew and Luke has progressed, on the whole, on the assumption that the Two-Source Theory is correct. The apparent success of this kind of redaction-criticism, which was one of the most important enterprises in Gospel criticism in the latter half of the twentieth century, appears to corroborate its basic premises, the priority

of Mark and the existence of Q. There are, however, major difficulties with using this as an argument in favour of the existence of Q:

(a)   Those using this argument tend to state it in terms of the success of the Two-Source Theory generally and not in terms of Q specifically. This is problematic, for while an argument of this kind might legitimately be used in favour of Markan Priority, for which we have an extant text with which we can compare Matthew and Luke, it is much less straightforward to use it in favour of Q, which is hypothetical. As often, Q is allowed to piggy-back onto Markan Priority, and to gain credibility by association with it.

(b)   The Q theory gains an unfair advantage over the Farrer Theory here because it has, as an hypothetical document, a far greater degree of flexibility. When we work with Luke's knowledge of Matthew, we are always looking at comparison between known texts. But Q, by contrast, can be manipulated.

(c)   We only have any idea of the contents of Q by attempting to reconstruct the document. And the primary means by which Q is reconstructed is *by means of redaction-criticism*. There is thus an unavoidable circularity in using this argument in favour of the existence of Q—a tool that has been used to generate a document is said to corroborate the existence of the document that has been generated.

(d)   Also related is, once more, the issue of entrenchment. Repeated studies of Matthew and Luke assume Q, thereby making those studies normative. It does not take long before one of the very tools for the study of Matthew and Luke is Q. The argument from the status quo then becomes little more than an assertion about the status quo.

It appears, then, that of the several arguments that are put forward to defend the Q theory, not one of them is adequate to the task. Indeed, in several of these categories, we cannot help thinking that the evidence in favour of the alternative position, Luke's use of Matthew, is stronger. In themselves, though, the answers to these arguments are not enough. It is true that, in the absence of good arguments for Luke's independence from Matthew, we might find ourselves drawn towards the Farrer Theory, but what we would like ideally is some concrete evidence. Is there anything that points directly to Luke's use of Matthew? The good news is that there is plenty of evidence in favour of Luke's use of Matthew, evidence that is repeatedly underplayed, misconstrued or ignored in Gospel scholarship.

Summary

- *The argument from the success of redaction-criticism* is also unconvincing:
  - Sometimes Q is allowed to gain credibility by association with Markan Priority, for which this argument is more legitimately used.
  - As an hypothetical document, Q has a degree of flexibility that gives it an unfair advantage.
  - Since Q is reconstructed by means of redaction-criticism, it can become a circular argument to assert Q on the basis of redaction-criticism.
  - An inevitable entrenchment of Q occurs the more it is assumed.

3. *Evidence of Luke's Use of Matthew*

Speculation and critical reflection on Luke's potential objectives in reworking Matthew will sound hollow if we are short of positive evidence that Luke knew and used the Gospel of Matthew. The evidence under consideration in this final, major section of our journey through the maze is therefore of vital importance. For here we will be considering the grounds for believing that Luke was familiar with Matthew. The decisive evidence can be considered under four headings, three of which we have already encountered in other contexts. We will take the most well known of these first, the Minor Agreements between Matthew and Luke against Mark.

a. *The Minor Agreements*

If Luke is dependent on Matthew, we will expect him to show knowledge of Matthew not only in the Double Tradition passages, that is, those passages usually attributed to Q, but also in the Triple Tradition passages, that is, those passages where he is dependent on Mark. Even if Mark is his primary source for the Triple Tradition material (see above, Chapters 3–4), we will nevertheless expect him to show some knowledge of Matthew's versions of this same material. This is indeed what we find.

The term 'Minor Agreements' refers to those agreements between Luke and Matthew against Mark in the Triple Tradition material. Their importance as evidence for Luke's use of Matthew should not be underestimated. For if Luke sometimes agrees with Matthew against Mark in important ways, then Matthew and Luke were not written independently of one another. And if they were not written independently of one another, Q is no longer required to explain the Double Tradition material—for this, Luke can be dependent primarily on Matthew.[11]

There are many, many Minor Agreements between Matthew and Luke against Mark. A good number of them can easily be explained on the assumption that Matthew and Luke are independently redacting Mark, coinciding in their attempts to polish up his literary style, to alter his harsh view of the disciples, his less reverential view of Jesus and so on. However, there is an irresolvable rump of agreements that simply will not go away. One of the most interesting occurs in a passage to which we have referred already, when Jesus is being mocked:

Matthew 26.67-68	Mark 14.65	Luke 22.64
Then they spat into his face, and struck him; and some slapped him, saying, 'Prophesy to us, you Christ! *Who is it that struck you?'*	And some began to spit on him, and to cover his face, and to strike him, saying to him, 'Prophesy!' And the guards received him with blows.	Now the men who were holding Jesus mocked him and beat him; they also blindfolded him and asked him, 'Prophesy! *Who is it that struck you?'*

11. Frans Neirynck, has attempted to counter this argument by pointing out that if the Minor Agreements were to demonstrate subsidiary Lukan dependence on Matthew in the Triple Tradition, then by analogy they would only demonstrate subsidiary dependence on Matthew in the Double Tradition. In other words, Q could still be postulated as the main source for the Double Tradition material. However, this misses the fact that the Farrer Theory's argument from the Minor Agreements *is not and has never been an argument from analogy*. Rather, it is an attempt to point to concrete evidence of Luke's knowledge of Matthew, evidence that inevitably undermines the major premise of Q, which is that Matthew and Luke are independent of one another. For details see Goodacre, *Goulder and the Gospels*, pp. 126-29; for Frans Neirynck's most recent statement, see 'Goulder and the Minor Agreements', *ETL* 73 (1997), pp. 84-93.

The passage is a helpful one for several reasons. Since this passage
occurs in the Passion Narrative, the Minor Agreement cannot be due to
use of Q. Q does not have, according to any of its contemporary
defenders, a Passion Narrative. Moreover, five words in Greek, the
words here translated as *Who is it that struck you?*, occur in both
Matthew and Luke but not in Mark. One of the words, the verb *to strike*
(in Greek *paiein*) is rare—it occurs only here in Matthew and only here
in Luke. It is not, then, the kind of agreement for which common oral
tradition is likely to be an explanation.

The most obvious scenario is that Matthew is here typically attempting to clarify the rather darkly ironic Markan scene, in which Jesus is
taunted with the demand 'Prophesy!' as his tormentors are in the very
act of fulfilling his prophecy (see further above, p. 64). Luke then follows Matthew in adding the clarificatory words, betraying his knowledge of Matthew.

How do Q theorists deal with this evidence? On the whole, they are
troubled by it since they realize that it challenges the notion of Luke's
independence from Matthew, the premise behind the Q theory. The
leading defence here is that Matthew did not originally contain the
words *Who is it that struck you?* The theory is that these words were
added by Luke and that scribes of Matthew then interpolated them into
their versions of Matthew. This is a process known as 'conjectural
emendation', where a scholar proposes an emendation to the text with
no warrant anywhere in the textual tradition—no known text of Matthew is without these words. Conjectural emendation is usually practised sparingly by Gospel scholars, and it is particularly problematic
here, where the primary reason for practising it is to defend an already
troubled synoptic theory, the Q hypothesis.[12]

There is some further evidence from within the category of the
Minor Agreements that points not just to some contact between Matthew and Luke but specifically suggests the direction of dependence,
Luke's knowledge of Matthew. For there is a small rump of Minor
Agreements that bear the unmistakable marks of Matthew's characteristic style or vocabulary, indicating that Luke might have inadvertently
betrayed his knowledge of Matthew. Let us look at an example of this:

---

12. For further details on this, see my *Goulder and the Gospels*, pp. 101-107,
and the literature cited there.

Matthew 22.27	Mark 12.22	Luke 20.32
Later than all, the woman died.	Last of all also the woman died.	*Later* also the woman died.

This verse comes in a story in which some Sadducees question Jesus about the resurrection. The woman marries seven brothers in sequence, each of whom dies, and then at the end she dies herself. Where Mark expresses this by saying that she died 'last' (Greek *eschaton*), Matthew and Luke both use the word 'later' (Greek *hysteron*). Now this might not look, at first sight, particularly remarkable. But the interesting thing about the choice of this word is that it occurs regularly in Matthew—seven times—but never in Luke (or Acts) outside of this parallel with Matthew. Furthermore, it is a word that Matthew appears to use in a distinctive way, to mean the last in a series (cf. both Mt. 21.37 and 26.60-1). On another occasion he again writes 'later' (*hysteron*, Mt. 21.37) where Mark writes 'last' (*eschaton*, Mk 12.6). In other words, it seems likely that Matthew has made a change to his Markan source in characteristic Matthaean manner, and that Luke has followed him, inadvertently betraying to us that he knows Matthew.

Nevertheless, one difficulty remains. Are not these Minor Agreements problematic for the case against Q in that they are, on the whole, so very minor? Should we not, if the Farrer Theory is correct, expect some more substantial agreement between Matthew and Luke against Mark? Indeed we should, and the mistake made by those pressing the point is that there *is* evidence for more substantial agreement between Matthew and Luke against Mark, evidence that is ignored in this context because it is placed in a different category of its own, usually labelled 'Mark–Q overlap', and we will turn to this next.

Summary

- *The Minor Agreements between Matthew and Luke against Mark* point to Luke's knowledge of Matthew in the Triple Tradition material.
- *Strong Minor Agreements occur in the Passion Narrative*, where no one can appeal to influence from Q.

> • *Several Minor Agreements show the marks of Matthew's distinctive style*, suggesting that Matthew has modified Mark and that Luke has followed Matthew.

b. *Passages in Which Mark Is Not the Middle Term*
When we began exploring the maze, in Chapter 2, taking a basic itinerary of all the available data, we found that there was one interesting class of material that defied straightforward categorization. Several pericopae appeared to object to the standard rule that Mark is the middle term. These pericopae did not allow themselves to be described either as Double Tradition (since they had parallels in Mark) or as Triple Tradition (since they featured major and not minor agreements between Matthew and Luke against Mark). Now another way of describing passages like this, in which Mark is not the middle term, is as pericopae occurring in all three Synoptics that feature substantial agreement between Matthew and Luke against Mark. This is a scenario that is problematic for the Q theory but highly congenial to the idea that Luke knew both Mark and Matthew and I will attempt to explain why.

First, this kind of passage is problematic for the Q theory because the material attributed to Q (i.e. the major agreements between Matthew and Luke against Mark) appears to presuppose the material present in Mark. This is much less congenial to the Q theory, which usually holds that Q was independent of Mark, than it is to the Farrer Theory, on which Matthew (and Luke) are presupposing Mark. To see the point, have a look again at one of the key 'Mark–Q overlap' passages, the John the Baptist complex:

Matthew 3.11-12	Mark 1.7-8	Luke 3.16-17
	7. 'And he preached, saying,	16. 'And John answered, saying to all,
11. '"I, *on the one hand*, baptize you in water for repentance, *but* the one who is coming after me is stronger than me, the shoes of whom I am not worthy to untie.	"The one who is stronger than me comes after me, the thong of whose sandals I am not worthy, having stooped down, to loose. 8.	"I, *on the one hand*, baptize you in water *but* the one who is stronger than me comes after me, the thong of whose sandals I am not worthy to loose.

	I baptized you in water [cf. Mt. 3.11//Lk. 3.16], but he will baptize you in holy spirit".'	
He will baptize you in holy spirit *and fire. 12. His winnowing fork is in his hand and he will clear his threshing floor and he will gather his wheat into his granary, but the chaff he will burn with unquenchable fire".'*		He will baptize you in holy spirit *and fire. 17. His winnowing fork is in his hand to clear his threshing floor and to gather the wheat into his granary, but the chaff he will burn with unquenchable fire".'*

Now what is so interesting here is the sheer degree of overlap between Mark and Q, overlap that amounts apparently to verbatim agreement between them. For we simply cannot imagine, for example, that Q just featured the words 'and fire' (Mt. 3.11//Lk. 3.16). These words require an antecedent, something exactly like 'he will baptize you in holy spirit', the very words that do appear in Mark (Mk 1.8 and parallels). On the Q theory, the Q document would appear to pre-suppose precisely the material that we can see to be present in Mark, which is more than a little odd if Mark and Q are (as most hold them to be) independent. On the Farrer Theory, by contrast, we can see Matthew simply presupposing his Markan source and elaborating on it, and subsequently getting followed by Luke. It is a much more straightforward theory.

There is, further, some additional corroboration for the Farrer Theory's perspective here. For if Matthew has added this fresh material to Mark, subsequently to be copied by Luke, we will expect the fresh material to feature some characteristically Matthaean language and themes. And this is exactly what we do find. For if any Gospel is particularly fond of the language of judgment, with Jesus separating the good and the evil, the wise and the foolish, the wheat and the weeds, often expressed using harvest imagery, it is Matthew's (cf., for example, Mt. 7.16-20; 12.33-37; 13.24-30, 36-43, 47-50; 25.31-46). It would be entirely in character here for Matthew to have introduced elements like judgment, separation and hell-fire.

But the existence of these passages is further troubling for Q because they contradict the assertion that Matthew and Luke only agree together against Mark in minor ways. This is important because it is sometimes said that the problem with the Minor Agreements (see

above) is that they are 'too minor' to make the case for Luke's use of
Matthew strongly enough. We need to see that this is simply not the
case—there are several passages that feature major agreements between
Matthew and Luke against Mark. Similarly, as we saw above, the
existence of these passages simply contradicts one of the major arguments for Q, that Luke never takes over Matthew's additions to Mark
in Triple Tradition material.

Along with the Minor Agreements on the one side and the 'pure
Triple Tradition' passages on the other side, this kind of passage
establishes the existence of a continuum that makes good sense on the
Farrer Theory, for if Luke has both Mark and Matthew as primary
sources, we will expect this to have resulted in a sliding scale of
Matthaean influence on Luke, from pure Triple Tradition passages that
feature Minor Agreements, to Mark–Q overlap passages that feature
major agreements between Matthew and Luke against Mark, to Double
Tradition passages where Luke is dependent solely on Matthew. We
might represent this scenario as in Fig. 4:

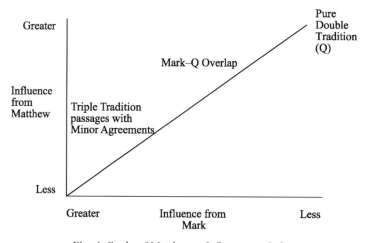

Fig. 4. *Scale of Matthaean Influence on Luke*

Here we note that there is a continuum in Luke's use of Mark and
Matthew, from passages where Luke is primarily dependent on Mark,
with only minor or subsidiary influence from Matthew, to passages
where Luke is more strongly influenced by Matthew (the so-called
'Mark–Q overlap' passages currently under discussion) to passages
where Luke has Matthew as his sole source ('pure Double Tradition' or

'Q' passages). In short, the existence of these passages causes some major difficulties for the Q theory while they are precisely what we would expect if Luke has used both Mark and Matthew.

Summary

- *Major agreements between Matthew and Luke against Mark*: although commonly placed in a category of their own labelled 'Mark–Q overlap', the difficulty these passages pose for the Q theory should not be underestimated:
  - They contradict the assertion that Luke never features Matthew's modifications of Mark in Triple Tradition material.
  - They illustrate the mid point on a continuum of Luke's use of Matthew, from greater (pure Double Tradition) to lesser (Triple Tradition).

---

c. *The Narrative Element in Q*

It is commonly said that Q provides us with a 'sayings source' or a 'Sayings Gospel' in which there is 'no narrative frame'. At first sight, this indeed seems to be the case: we saw when first exploring the maze, for example, that much of the Double Tradition material is sayings material—beatitudes, parables, aphorisms, exhortation and teaching material of different kinds. But on closer inspection, we find something very revealing, evidence that suggests that we should be cautious over talking about Q as a 'sayings source' or a 'Sayings Gospel', evidence that points, once more, to the plausibility of the Farrer Theory.

The feature of Q that is not commonly noticed is that its first third apparently has a marked narrative sequence in which the progress of Jesus' ministry is carefully plotted. In outline the sequence goes as follows:

(a)   John the Baptist appears in the region of the Jordan (Mt. 3.6//Lk. 3.3).

(b)   John baptizes people with 'his baptism' (Mt. 3.7//Lk. 3.7), a baptism apparently connected with 'repentance' (Mt. 3.8//Lk. 3.8).

(c)   John preaches about a 'coming one' (Mt. 3.11//Lk. 3.16).

(d) Jesus appears on the scene and there is a baptism involving the 'spirit' in which Jesus is recognized as a 'son' (Mt. 3.13-17//Lk. 3.21-22).

(e) Jesus is led into the wilderness by 'the spirit' to be tested as 'son' (Mt. 4.1-11//Lk. 4.1-13).

(f) Jesus appears in a place called 'Nazara' (Mt. 4.13//Lk. 4.16).

(g) Jesus preaches a great Sermon (Mt. 5–7//Lk. 6.20-49).

(h) Jesus finishes his Sermon and goes to Capernaum where a Centurion's Boy is healed (Mt. 7.28-29; 8.5//Lk. 7.1).

(i) Messengers come from John the Baptist, asking whether Jesus is indeed 'the coming one' (Mt. 11.2-19//Lk. 7.18-35).[13]

One of the most interesting features of this is that it seems to be a *narrative* sequence—each event clearly proceeds from the previous one. John appears, preaches about his baptism, prophesies 'the coming one', who then appears, is baptized in connection with the 'spirit' as a 'son', is then led by the 'spirit' to be tested as a 'son' and so on. This is problematic for the Q theory in two ways. First, it contradicts the assertion that Q is a 'Sayings Gospel' or 'sayings source' without narrative frame. An extant example of a genuine 'Sayings Gospel' has come to light this century, the Gospel of Thomas, a full copy of which was discovered in Nag Hammadi, Egypt, in 1945. The disappointing news for the Q theory is that the document looks nothing like Q as it is commonly reconstructed. Thomas is quite lacking in the kind of ordered arrangements that characterize Q, especially the all-important narrative sequence in Q's first third. Thus, far from corroborating the existence of documents like Q, the blatant contrast between Thomas and Q gives one major pause for thought.

This contrast is intensified by the fact that it finds a ready explanation on the Farrer Theory. Q's narrative sequence makes sense when

13. Please note that I am not here maximizing material that might be attributed to Q. Rather, I have only mentioned material that is agreed to belong to Q by the International Q Project, whose critical text of Q is the end result of over ten years of hard work by experts in the area. For example, the sharp eye will notice that items (a) to (e) are partly 'Mark–Q overlap' material discussed above. In deference to the experts, I have only included Mark–Q overlap material that occurs in the International Q Project's critical text. See James M. Robinson, Paul Hoffmann and John S. Kloppenborg (eds.), *The Critical Edition of Q: Synopsis Including the Gospels of Matthew and Luke, Mark and Thomas, with English, German and French Translations of Q and Thomas* (Minneapolis, MN: Fortress Press; Leuven: Peeters, 2000).

one notices that it corresponds to the places at which Matthew departs from Mark's basic order (in Mt. 3–11) and where Luke, in parallel, also departs from that order (in Lk. 1–9). In other words, the narrative sequence is generated by a feature in the structuring of the Gospels. On the whole, Matthew departs regularly from Mark in the first third of his Gospel (Mt. 3–11), restructuring and adding fresh material to the Markan outline, but he is much more conservative with Mark's order in his second two-thirds.

If a further indication was needed, we might notice that at least one of the elements in this narrative sequence bears the unmistakable mark of Matthew's hand:

Matthew 7.28-29; 8.5	*Luke 7.1*
And it came to pass that when Jesus had completed these words, the crowds were amazed at his teaching… and when he had entered into Capernaum, a centurion came…	When Jesus had fulfilled all these sayings in the hearing of the people, he entered into Capernaum. And a certain Centurion's Servant…

What is so striking about this narrative segue, absent of course from Mark, is that it is well known as Matthew's own particular formula. It is the form of words he uses every time he ends one of his five major discourses, here (the Sermon on the Mount) and then again on these four occasions:

Mt. 11.1:   'After Jesus had finished instructed his twelve disciples…'
Mt. 13.53:   'When Jesus had finished these parables…'
Mt. 19.1:   'When Jesus had finished saying these things…'
Mt. 26.1:   'When Jesus had finished saying all these things…'

In short, it seems that once again we can detect Matthew's hand in what is normally held to be material derived from Q. The narrative sequence seen in the standard reconstructions of Q's first third is highly congenial to the Farrer Theory but is problematic for Q.

Summary

- The Q material seems to exhibit *a narrative sequence*, found especially in the first third of the alleged document:

- This contrasts with markedly with anything in the one extant example we have of a Sayings Gospel, the Coptic Gospel of Thomas.
- It makes good sense on the assumption that it is generated by Luke's use of non-Markan material in Matthew's Gospel, the first third of which often departs from Mark.
- Elements in the narrative sequence show the clear signs of Matthew's redactional hand.

d. *Editorial Fatigue*

When we were looking at the Priority of Mark in Chapter 3 we found one of the most decisive factors to be the phenomenon of 'editorial fatigue'. There were places where Matthew and Luke seemed to have made initial, characteristic changes to their Markan source, but had then apparently lapsed into docile reproduction of that source, resulting in some minor incongruities. Now it is revealing that the same phenomenon also seems to occur in the Double Tradition, revealing because it is always in the same direction, in favour of Luke's use of Matthew. As usual, illustration will be the best form of explanation, so let us have a look at a good example, the Parable of the Talents/Pounds (Mt. 25.14-30//Lk. 19.11-27).

When I was at school, the Matthaean version of this parable was always the one read in assembly, partly because it had the desired word 'talent' in it (we needed to be encouraged to 'use our talents', that is, to play in the school band, to act in the school play or to play for the school football team), but also because it is the simpler, more coherent, easier to follow version. There are three servants; one receives five talents, one two and the other one. The first makes five more talents and is rewarded, the second two more and is rewarded; the other hides his talent and is punished.

By contrast, the Lukan version begins with ten servants, all of whom receive one pound. It is an adjustment typical of Luke, the evangelist most fond of the ratio of ten to one (ten coins, one lost in Lk. 15.8-10; ten lepers, one thankful, in Lk. 17.11-17, and so on). However, when the nobleman returns, he summons the servants, and, instead of hearing about the ten earlier mentioned, we hear about 'the first' (Lk. 19.16), 'the second' (Lk. 19.18) and amazingly, 'the other' (Greek *ho heteros*, Lk. 19.20). It turns out, then, that Luke has three servants in mind, like Matthew, and not ten after all. Further, in Luke's parable, the first two servants receive 'cities' as their reward (19.17, 19), the first ten and the second five, whereas in Matthew they are 'put in charge of much' (25.21, 23). Yet towards the end of the parable, Luke seems to corroborate not his own earlier story line but Matthew's:

Matthew 25.28	Luke 19.24
'So take the talent from him and give it to him who has the ten talents'.	'Take the pound from him and give it to him who has the ten pounds'.

The account lacks cohesion: the man in Luke actually has ten cities now, so a pound extra is nothing and, in any case, he does not have ten pounds but eleven (19.16: 'your pound made ten pounds more'; contrast Mt. 25.20).

Luke's version of the parable, then, does not hold together well and there is a straightforward explanation to hand: Luke has attempted to reframe Matthew's parable but editorial fatigue leads him to drift into the story line of his Matthaean source, inadvertently betraying his knowledge of Matthew.

Nor is this parable an isolated example—there are several clear cases of Double Tradition material in which Luke appears to show editorial fatigue in his copying of Matthew, as when he begins talking about the Centurion's 'slave' (Greek *doulos*, Lk. 7.2; cf. 7.10) in contrast to Matthew's Centurion's 'son' or 'servant' (Greek *pais*, Mt. 8.6), only subsequently to drift into Matthew's wording (*pais*, Mt. 8.8//Lk. 7.7). Or one might look at Lk. 9.5 in which Jesus speaks about when the disciples leave 'that town'. No town has been mentioned in the previous verses, Lk. 9.1-6 (Mission Charge, cf. Mk 6.6b-13//Mt. 10.5-15). It seems, then, that Luke has copied the words from Matthew (10.14), who does have the appropriate antecedent (Mt. 10.11, 'and whatever town or village you enter…').

It could, of course, be the case that Luke is simply fatigued in such cases with a Q source better represented by Matthew. The difficulty with this idea, however, is that it seems impossible to find reverse examples, cases where Matthew has apparently become fatigued with Q, something that would be very odd given his clear tendency to become fatigued in his copying of Mark (see above, Chapter 3). This is more evidence, then, that the Double Tradition material is due not to Matthew's and Luke's independent copying of Q but rather to Luke's use of Matthew.

Summary

- Just as there appear to be cases where Matthew and Luke become fatigued in their versions of Triple Tradition (copying from Mark), so too there appear to be cases where Luke becomes fatigued in his copying of material in the Double Tradition.
- Since there are no counter-examples of apparent Matthaean fatigue in Double Tradition material, the obvious explanation is that Luke becomes fatigued not with Q but with Matthew.

4. *Conclusion*

a. *Summary*

As we draw to the end of our journey through the maze, in this, that longest chapter so far, we have looked at the case against the existence of Q. This has been a two-part process:

(a)   *The standard arguments for existence of Q appear to be inadequate*—indeed close consideration of them in each case leads us directly to the plausibility of Luke's use of Matthew:

1.   *Luke's order*: It is commonly said that Luke's order of Double Tradition material is inexplicable on the assumption that he has taken this material from Matthew. However, this runs into the following difficulties:

   - *Dubious value judgments*: The standard argument assumes that Matthew's arrangement of Double Tradition, with its lengthy discourses, is preferable to Luke's with its emphasis on narrative movement, but this is an unnecessary, subjective assumption.
   - *Redaction-criticism of Luke's use of Mark*: Luke treats Matthew's lengthy discourses in the same way that he treats Mark's discourses: he keeps some, omits some and redistributes the rest.
   - *Narrative-criticism of Luke*: This helps us to dispense with the idea that Matthew's arrangements are superior to Luke's—Luke's rearrangements make excellent narrative-critical sense.
   - *Luke's preface*: Luke 1.1-4 implies a critical attitude to his predecessors' *order*. This critical attitude makes good

sense on the assumption that Luke is working with Matthew as well as Mark.

- *Markan Priority*: If Luke has known Mark for longer than he has known Matthew, this may well have encouraged him to prioritize its order over Matthew's.

2. *Luke's ignorance of Matthew's additions to Mark*: this argument runs into insurmountable problems:

   - *Strength of evidence*: The examples given are not strong enough to make the case. Luke's omissions are quite natural when one looks at them in line with his redactional interests.
   - *Fallacious argument*: The argument is based on a fallacy: wherever Luke features Matthew's additions to Mark, these are placed in the category 'Mark–Q overlap' and ignored for the purposes of this argument.

3. *Luke's lack of 'M' material*: Luke lacks Matthew's Special Material by definition—where Matthew's non-Marcan material appears in Luke, it is called 'Double Tradition'. Further:

   - *Matthew's Birth Narrative*: There are signs that Luke knows the narrative even though he does not utilise it extensively.
   - *'M' material*: The 'M' material all looks like 'Luke-displeasing' material, just what we would expect on the Farrer Theory.

4. *Alternating Primitivity*: A phenomenon that can be explained in the following steps:

   - *Lukan secondariness*: There are many places where all agree that Luke is secondary.
   - *Matthaean language*: The presence of Matthew's favourite expressions in Q material is regularly taken to indicate that his versions are later than Luke's versions. But the same evidence is congenial to the thesis that Luke is using Matthew: Matthew composes the non-Markan material using characteristic expressions and Luke sometimes eliminates such expressions. Moreover, Luke has a much larger vocabulary than Matthew and he uses many more unusual expressions. It is a fallacy to assume that 'un-Lukan' expressions are necessarily 'pre-Lukan' expressions.

- *Neglected arguments for Lukan secondariness*: Sometimes scholars have drastically underestimated the arguments for Luke's redaction of Matthew (e.g. the Beatitudes).
- *Oral tradition*: The living stream of oral tradition did not dry up as soon as the evangelists set pen to papyrus. Just as Matthew creatively interacted with Mark in the light of oral traditions, so too did Luke with Matthew and Mark.

5. *The Distinctiveness of Q*: Here the following points are relevant:

- *Isolation of Double Tradition from its context*: this isolation of the Double Tradition from its context in Matthew and Luke inevitably generates a distinctive profile for Q.
- *Overlap between Q and M*: this overlap between Q material and M material partly undermines the claim.
- *L Material*: it is difficult to discover good candidates for material that might have derived from Q among Luke's special material.
- *A Distinctive Profile*: the Double Tradition has a distinctive profile on the Farrer Theory, namely (Matthew *minus* Mark) *divided by* 'Luke-pleasingness'.

6. *The Redaction-critical Argument*:

- *Association with Markan Priority*: Q is allowed to gain credibility by association with Markan Priority, for which this argument is more legitimately used.
- *Flexibility of Q*: As an hypothetical document, Q has a degree of flexibility that gives it an unfair advantage.
- *Redaction-criticism*: Since Q is reconstructed by means of Redaction-Criticism, it is circular to argue in favour of Q on the basis of redaction-criticism.
- *Entrenchment*: an inevitable entrenchment of Q occurs the more it is assumed.

(b) *Direct evidence*: There is direct evidence for Luke's use of Matthew, evidence that on the whole has been ignored or explained away:

1. *Minor Agreements between Matthew and Luke against Mark*: These seem to point to Luke's knowledge of Matthew in the Triple Tradition material:

- *Passion Narrative*: Strong Minor Agreements occur in the Passion Narrative, where no one can appeal to influence from Q.
- *Matthew's Style*: Several Minor Agreements show the marks of Matthew's distinctive style, suggesting that he was the composer of this material.

2. *Major Agreements between Matthew and Luke against Mark*: Although commonly placed in a category of their own labelled 'Mark–Q overlap', the difficulty these passages pose for the Q theory should not be underestimated:
    - *Contradiction*: They contradict the assertion that Luke never features Matthew's modifications of Mark in Triple Tradition material.
    - *Continuum*: They illustrate the mid point on a continuum of Luke's use of Matthew and Mark, from greater (pure Double Tradition) to lesser (Triple Tradition).

3. *Narrative Sequence in the Q material*: This is found especially in the first third of the alleged document:
    - *Contrast with Thomas*: The narrative sequence contrasts with anything found in the one extant example we have of a Sayings Gospel, the Coptic Gospel of Thomas.
    - *Non-Markan narrative in Matthew*: The narrative sequence makes good sense on the assumption that it is generated by Luke's following the non-Markan material in Matthew, the first third of which often departs from Mark.
    - *Matthew's Redactional Hand*: Elements in the narrative sequence show the clear signs of Matthew's redactional hand.

4. *Editorial fatigue*:
    - *The Double Tradition*: Just as there appear to be cases where Matthew and Luke become fatigued in their versions of Triple Tradition (copying from Mark), so too there appear to be cases where Luke becomes fatigued in his copying of material in the Double Tradition.
    - *No Counter-Examples*: Since there are no counter-examples of apparent Matthaean fatigue in Double Tradition material, the obvious explanation is that Luke became fatigued not with Q but with Matthew.

b. *Occam's Razor*

Having earlier accepted the theory of Markan Priority as by far the best explanation of much of the data, we find at the end of this chapter that we are left with two competing theories that build on Markan Priority in order to explain the remainder of the data. We have a problematic theory in which the existence of an hypothetical document, Q, is postulated, and an unproblematic one in which it is not. Under such circumstances, we are left with little choice but to appeal to an old principle known as *Occam's Razor*. The British mediaeval philosopher William of Occam suggested a fine working principle: that entities should not be multiplied beyond what is necessary.[14] In other words, there is no point in continuing to appeal to an hypothetical document to explain data that is better explained without it. Or to put it another way, the plausibility of the theory of Luke's use of Matthew enables us to dispense with Q.

Many scholars naturally balk at this suggestion because Q has been an important part of the landscape of New Testament scholarship for a long time. A great deal has been staked in Q. Books and articles continue to be produced in abundance. Scholars continue to appeal to Q to help them to reconstruct the life of the historical Jesus and to explore Christian origins. But attachment to the familiar because it is familiar, and fondness for an entity that has been honoured by time, should play no role in helping us to make our mind up about the Synoptic Problem. If the evidence demands that we dispense with Q, then that is what we will have to do.

There are, however, important compensations that make taking leave of Q worth the pain that is inevitably generated by the break-up. For one thing, it enables us to be people of the twenty-first century. It is arguable that Q belongs to another age, an age in which scholars solved every problem by postulating another written source. The evangelists were thought of as 'scissors and paste' men, compilers and not composers, who edited together pieces from several documents. Classically, the bookish B.H. Streeter solved the Synoptic Problem by assigning a written source to each type of material—Triple Tradition was from Mark; Double Tradition was from 'Q'; special Matthew was from 'M' and special Luke was from 'L'. It is now rare to see scholars appealing

---

14. The Latin formulation is *entia non sunt multiplicanda praeter necessitatem*, 'entities should not be multiplied without necessity'.

to written 'M' and 'L' documents. Perhaps at last the time has come to get up to date, and to dispense with Q too.

This brings with it the advantage to which we have alluded several times in this chapter, that dispensing with Q allows us to appreciate the evangelists' literary ability. Q has caused many scholars to be unduly obsessed with the isolation of the precise wording of Matthew's and Luke's hypothetical source, leading them away from a full appreciation of the way in which they creatively interacted with Mark, the Hebrew Bible and the living stream of oral tradition. The impediment provided by Q to the proper appreciation of Luke's literary ability is felt particularly strongly. His distinctive ordering of the Double Tradition material has traditionally been explained on the assumption that he was conservatively following a Q text. But, as we have begun to see, it is quite conceivable that Luke should have imaginatively and creatively re-ordered material from Matthew. Luke avoids his predecessor's more rigid, thematic approach in order to develop a plausible, sequential narrative of the events he sees as having been fulfilled in the midst of his readers.

Chapter 7

EMERGING FROM THE MAZE

The journey is almost over. It is time to emerge from the maze. Let us review our way through it.

1. *Preliminaries*

The fundamental presupposition for the study of the Synoptic Problem is that there is a distinction between Matthew, Mark and Luke, on the one hand, and John, on the other. Once one has arranged Matthew, Mark and Luke in a *Synopsis*, these *Synoptic Gospels* can be seen to have a literary interrelationship. The *Synoptic Problem* is all about working out precisely what kind of relationship is involved.

2. *Types of Material*

The use of the Synopsis enables one to work out the different kinds of material present in the Synoptic Gospels. Broadly speaking, there are four different kinds of material: *Triple Tradition* (shared by Matthew, Mark and Luke), *Double Tradition* (shared by Matthew and Luke alone), *Special Matthew* (material only in Matthew) and *Special Luke* (material only in Luke). To arrive at a solution to the Synoptic Problem, one needs to account plausibly for the origins of these different strands of material, especially the material shared by two or more Gospels. The common explanation for the origin of Triple Tradition is the theory of *Markan Priority*, the idea that Mark was the first of the Gospels to have been written and that it was used by both Matthew and Luke, who in this material copied from Mark.

3. *Markan Priority*

For a variety of reasons, Markan Priority emerges as the most plausible, major element in the solution to the Synoptic Problem. Its main rival, the theory of Markan Posteriority (the *Griesbach Theory*), whereby Mark makes direct use of both Matthew and Luke, is less plausible. Markan Posteriority, for example, requires Mark to have made substantial omissions of congenial material from Matthew and Luke at the expense of adding material of an almost banal clarificatory nature, additions that do not seem consonant with his concern elsewhere to create a darkly ironic, mysterious narrative. Mark has too many 'harder readings' for Markan Posteriority to be plausible, and where there are indications of dates, the indications are that Matthew and Luke postdate the fall of Jerusalem in 70 CE, whereas Mark does not. There seem, further, to be clear cases of Matthew and Luke becoming 'fatigued' in their copying of units from Mark, making characteristic changes at the beginning of pericopae and not managing to sustain such changes throughout.

4. *Two-Source Theory or Farrer?*

But once one has decided in favour of Markan Priority, one needs to ask a second key question: Did Matthew and Luke use Mark independently of one another or are there signs that one of them also knew the other? The standard position, The *Two-Source Theory*, maintains that Matthew and Luke were indeed *independent* of one another. This means that the only possible explanation for the Double Tradition material, in which there is major agreement between Matthew and Luke, is that they were both dependent on an otherwise unknown source, for convenience called *Q*. However the standard arguments for the Q hypothesis are weak, and the *Farrer Theory*, which maintains both Markan Priority and Luke's knowledge of Matthew, is preferable.

It is commonly said, for example, that Luke's order of the Double Tradition material is inexplicable on the assumption that he has taken it from Matthew. But such a perspective does not take seriously Luke's desire to interweave sayings material with narrative in order to create a plausible, sequential account, rather than to have gigantic monologues of the kind Matthew favours. To give another example, it is commonly said that Luke shows no knowledge of any of the Matthaean additions to Mark in Triple Tradition material, something that is manifestly not the case. Matthew's additions to John the Baptist's preaching, for example, with their characteristic Matthean emphases, are reproduced verbatim in Luke.

Indeed, the value of the Farrer Theory is that it is able to point to strong evidence that Luke knew not only Mark but also Matthew's version of Mark. Both the Minor Agreements and the Major Agreements between Matthew and Luke against Mark (the Major Agreements are more commonly called 'Mark–Q overlap') are thorns in the side of the Q theory, for they seem to present evidence that Luke knows Matthew's specific modifications of the Markan material. Where Jesus is being mocked, in Mark he is simply told to 'Prophesy!' (Mk 14.65), a darkly ironic taunt from those who are in the very act of fulfilling Jesus' prophecy that he will be struck and spat upon. Matthew typically explicates and simplifies the ironic scene by adding a five word question, 'Who is it who smote you?', and he is followed by Luke, as clear a sign as one could want that Luke knows Matthew.

Further, the Farrer Theory explains plausibly elements of editorial fatigue that appear in Luke over against Matthew, like the disappearance of seven of Luke's ten servants in the Parable of the Pounds. And it makes good sense of the clearly traceable narrative sequence that makes up the early part of the Double Tradition in both Matthew and Luke, a narrative sequence that contradicts the standard characterization of 'Q' as a 'Sayings Gospel', and which presupposes elements in the Triple Tradition, a sign that the material was crafted by someone like Matthew for this very narrative context.

5. *What Makes a Good Solution?*

The ideal solution to the Synoptic Problem is one that is able explain the origin and nature of all three Synoptics in the most plausible way. The solution proposed here helps one to reflect critically on the growth of the Gospel genre and the development of early Christianity. If one assumes the Farrer Theory, whereby Mark writes first, Matthew writes in interaction with Mark and Luke writes in interaction with both, the following, plausible scenario emerges. Of all the Gospels, Mark's is the one that makes the most sense as standing at the genesis of the Gospel genre. If Mark's Gospel was written first, he was the first to forge together oral traditions concerning the life of Jesus into a story beginning with John the Baptist and culminating with the Passion and Resurrection. Mark was therefore generated by the evangelist's desire to marry disparate materials concerning Jesus' life with his fervent belief, no doubt influenced by acquaintance with Paul and Paulinism, that the

Crucified Christ is the heart of the good news about Jesus Christ, which should be at the centre of Christian faith.

Matthew partly embraces and partly reacts against Mark. It is the first attempt to 'fix' what he sees as lacking, both in content and outlook, in Mark's Gospel, thus 'drawing from the treasure both new and old' (Mt. 13.52). Matthew thus reinscribes Jesus' Jewish identity, making much more explicit use of the motif of Old Testament fulfilment, enhancing the role of Jesus the teacher, systematically explicating and ironing out the Markan oddities, and adding a birth and infancy narrative at one end and more resurrection material at the other end.

Luke, who has already known Mark for some years, comes across a copy of Matthew and can see immediately what it is—an attempt to 'fix' Mark in the ways just mentioned. This provides Luke with a catalyst—it gives him the idea of trying to improve on Mark himself, imitating Matthew's grand plan but at the same time attempting to better it. Thus Luke, like Matthew, writes a new version of Mark, making it a similar length to Matthew's Gospel, framing it in the same way, with birth narratives at the beginning and resurrection stories at the end, and in between adding a substantial amount of sayings material as well as some more fresh narrative. As Luke, like Matthew, attempts to fix Mark, he utilizes many of Matthew's own materials to do the job, especially the rich quarry of sayings material. But not for Luke are huge monologues like the Sermon on the Mount. He is attempting to write a plausible, sequential narrative of 'the events that have been fulfilled among us' (1.1) and this means avoiding Matthew's wooden structures, instead choosing to interweave deeds and sayings and to create a feeling of movement and progress, a progress that is not halted until, at the end of his second volume (the Acts of the Apostles), Paul is in Rome.

The advantage that the Farrer Theory has over its rivals is that it can provide a strong reason for the genesis of each of the Synoptic Gospels. The Synoptics turn out not only to provide source material for one another, Mark for Matthew and both for Luke, but also to be catalysts for one another, Mark for Matthew and both for Luke. Mark makes good sense as the first Gospel; Matthew makes good sense on the assumption that it represents a reaction against, and to some extent an embracing of, Mark. Luke makes fine sense on the assumption that it imitates but also improves on Matthew, utilizing some of his very material. By contrast, the other major theories have difficulties here.

The Griesbach Theory struggles to explain the genesis of Mark on the assumption that the evangelist is conflating Matthew and Luke—it is not easy to see why, on this theory, Mark would have written this book, and why, having chosen to write it, he creates a book that is so ill at ease with its own editorial policy, sometimes pushing in one direction, sometimes going in another. Likewise, the Two-Source Theory has trouble explaining how Matthew and Luke independently came up with the same plan at the same time but in ignorance of one another, both deciding to produce a fresh version of Mark, of the same length, framed in the same way, adding much of the same substance, often making similar alterations. Of course it is possible that they did indeed hit on the same plan at just the same time, but all in all it is not as satisfactory or as plausible a theory as one that assumes that one was the direct catalyst for the other. In the end, we should settle for the theory that has the fewest problems.

6. The Future

What, though, is the future for the study of the Synoptic Problem? Will it be abandoned by scholars who see it as too complex and too dull or is there hope for a brighter future? While making predictions is danger-ous, there are several avenues that might be explored further, which suggests that there are still reasons to be optimistic. First, it would be encouraging to see scholars dispensing with wooden models in which the evangelists remain scissors-and-paste people in favour of a proper appreciation of their literary abilities. This goal may be on its way to being achieved in that recent years have seen many useful literary-critical appreciations of individual Gospels. The rise of the discipline known as 'narrative-criticism', whereby a book's narrative is carefully analysed on its own terms, without recourse to theories about seams and sources, can only help scholars of the Synoptic Problem to pay more attention to the literary artistry that is such a major element in the Gospels, books that have, after all, enchanted generations of readers.

Second, recent scholarship has paid much more attention to the role played by oral tradition in Christian origins. Where scholars in the past have tended to paint the evangelists in their own image, as bookish people writing in their studies, primarily using literary resources, future scholars may well attempt to appreciate more accurately the way that the evangelists dealt with their materials. If we take all the evidence seriously, from Luke's Preface (Lk. 1.1-4) onwards, we cannot avoid the conclusion that the evangelists were involved in a creative, critical interaction with oral traditions as well as with literary sources.

Third, it would be a wonderful thing if interest in the Synoptic Problem could be refreshed and so restored to a place of prominence and interest within New Testament scholarship. In recent times it has become stagnant, often regarded as one of the least exciting or profitable areas to research or study. Yet some contemporary developments within New Testament scholarship are highly congenial to a renaissance for the Synoptic Problem. The study of the New Testament in film and fiction, for example, is now a topic of interest to New Testament scholars, and here there is fertile ground for interaction with Synoptic Problem studies. Instead of engaging only with Luke's use of Matthew, why not also look at Pier Paolo Pasolini's treatment of the same source in the film *The Gospel According to St Matthew*? Who knows?—fresh conversation partners might have fresh insights to bring.

Finally, one of the recent advances in historical Jesus study is the attempt to push back canonical boundaries. The canonical Gospels, Matthew, Mark, Luke and John, should not be privileged as historical sources purely by virtue of their inclusion in the canon. Scholars are now recognizing that they should at least be open to the possibility that reliable material about the historical Jesus might be located in other, non-canonical sources. It might also be a good idea to take non-canonical sources seriously in the study of the Synoptic Problem, not least because of the discovery in 1945 in Nag Hammadi, Egypt, of a complete Gospel in Coptic with many parallels to the Synoptic Gospels, a Gospel that must have been written by the end of the second century, and that may well be earlier. The question of the dating and reliability of Thomas as a source for very early Jesus material is controversial, but one thing is clear—studying its parallels with the Synoptic Gospels is rewarding and it may well end up shedding some fresh light on the Synoptic Problem.

Whatever the future holds for the Synoptic Problem, though, it is clear that it remains worthy of continued attention. Those who take time to reflect on it find the Synoptic Problem an enormously rewarding and still crucial area of New Testament studies. Indeed, for as long as it is called a 'problem' in need of a solution, scholars and students will persist in talking to each other about Jesus, the Gospels and Christian origins, continuing a conversation that has already begun within the canon of the New Testament itself. For when we look at the Gospels side by side, it is difficult to avoid asking fascinating questions about the similarities and differences, the tensions and interactions, between Mark, who gives us 'the beginning of the Gospel of Jesus Christ' (Mk 1.1), Matthew, who 'draws from his treasure chest both the new and the old' (Mt. 13.52) and Luke, who has 'investigated every-thing carefully from the beginning' in order to reassure Theophilus of 'the truth concerning the things about which he has been instructed' (Lk. 1.1-4). Our choice is to ignore that conversation, taking refuge in a harmonizing process that robs the texts of their individuality, or to take the agreements and the disagreements seriously, engaging in a critical discussion that has the potential not only to be educational but also, in the end, to be fun.

FURTHER READING

1. *Texts and Synopses*

If you have enjoyed finding your way through the maze, you will want to do some more reading. The most important thing is to read the Gospels themselves. If you know Greek, or are planning to learn Greek, get hold of a Greek New Testament as soon as you can, ideally *Novum Testamentum Graece* (Nestle–Aland 27th edition, 1993). If you can't find one in the shops, you can get hold of it from your local Bible Society (details on the web at http.//www.biblesociety.org). If you are planning to use an English translation, the most popular one among scholars is probably the *New Revised Standard Version*. But other useful translations include the *New International Version*, the *New American Standard Version*, the *Revised Standard Version* and the *New Jerusalem Bible*. You might also want to look at the many available on-line Bible versions and translations—for details go to *The New Testament Gateway* at http://www.NTGateway.com.

There is one thing, however, that is key to grasping the Synoptic Problem and that is to get hold of a Synopsis of the Gospels. If you have Greek, there are two possibilities, the first of which is now much more popular among scholars than the second:

Kurt Aland, *Synopsis Quattuor Evangeliorum* (Stuttgart: Deutsche Bibelgesellschaft, 15th edn, 1996, 1997).

Albert Huck, *Synopsis of the First Three Gospels* (fundamentally revised by Heinrich Greeven; Tübingen: J.C.B. Mohr [Paul Siebeck], 13th edn, 1981).

If you would like a combined Greek and English Synopsis:

K. Aland (ed.), *Synopsis of the Four Gospels* (Greek/English; Stuttgart: Deutsche Bibelgesellschaft, 10th edn, 1994).

Or, for purely English Synopses there are two main options:

K. Aland (ed.), *Synopsis of the Four Gospels* (English; Stuttgart: Deutsche Bibelgesellschaft, 1985).

Burton H. Throckmorton, Jr, *Gospel Parallels: A Comparison of the Synoptic Gospels* (Nashville, TN: Thomas Nelson, 1993).

If you cannot find them in the shops, you should be able to find the Aland Synopses at your local Bible Society (see http://www. biblesociety.org).

2. *Some Useful Literature*

William Farmer, *The Gospel of Jesus: The Pastoral Relevance of the Synoptic Problem* (Louisville, KY: Westminster/John Knox Press, 1994). This is probably the best place to go to get a handle on the Griesbach Theory, written by its chief exponent.

Michael Goulder, *Luke: A New Paradigm* (JSNTSup, 20; Sheffield: Sheffield Academic Press, 1989). Extensive and always engaging exposition of Luke's Gospel from the Farrer theory's leading exponent.

Peter Head, *Christology and the Synoptic Problem: An Argument for Markan Priority* (SNTSMS, 94; Cambridge: Cambridge University Press, 1997). Head's book is one of the best books recently published on the Synoptic Problem. It takes two theories, Two-Source and Griesbach, and looks at how plausible they are in using specific themes and passages connected with Christology.

Luke Johnson, *The Writings of the New Testament* (Minneapolis: Augsburg–Fortress; London: SCM Press, rev. edn, 1999 [1986]). Lucid introduction to each book in the New Testament, Johnson's book has established itself as a key student textbook.

J. Kloppenborg Verbin, *Excavating Q: The History and Setting of the Sayings Gospel* (Minneapolis: Augsburg–Fortress; Edinburgh: T. & T. Clark, 2000). Latest book from one of the leading international defenders of the Q hypothesis.

Helmut Koester, *Ancient Christian Gospels: Their History and Development* (London: SCM Press; Valley Forge, PA: Trinity Press International, 1990). Fascinating study that refuses to limit itself purely to canonical texts, Koester's book has discussions of all early Christian Gospels, including even fragmentary and hypothetical ones.

E.P. Sanders and M. Davies, *Studying the Synoptic Gospels* (London: SCM; Philadelphia: Trinity Press International, 1989). Introduction to key aspects of studying the Synoptics, including sections on the Synoptic Problem, form-criticism, redaction-criticism and historical Jesus research. An ideal student textbook.

Robert Stein, *The Synoptic Problem: An Introduction* (Grand Rapids: Baker Book House, 1987). Introduction to the Synoptic Problem written from the perspective of the Two-Source Theory.

Christopher Tuckett, *Q and the History of Early Christianity: Studies on Q* (Edinburgh: T. & T. Clark, 1996). Provides a defence of the Q theory and an extensive series of excellent studies on its place in early Christianity.

3. *On the World Wide Web*

For a directory of good, online resources on the Synoptic Problem, as well as for all other New Testament materials, visit *The New Testament Gateway* at http://www.NTGateway.com.

GLOSSARY

Double Tradition   Material that is found in both Matthew and Luke but not Mark. Sometimes called 'Q material' because of the alleged source of this material (q.v.).

Evangelists   In this context, the word 'evangelists' always refers to the authors of the Gospels and not to contemporary preachers. The evangelists are called for convenience Matthew, Mark, Luke and John without assuming necessarily that these were the names of the authors of the books that now bear those names.

Farrer Theory   Theory originating with Austin Farrer that Matthew used Mark and that Luke used Mark and Matthew. Also known as 'the Farrer–Goulder Theory', 'Mark-without-Q' and 'Markan Priority Without Q'.

J.J. Griesbach   (1745–1812). He produced the first Synopsis of the Gospels (q.v.) and the first critical solution to the Synoptic Problem, the Griesbach Hypothesis (q.v.).

Griesbach Theory   The theory that Matthew was the first Gospel, that Luke used Matthew and that Mark used them both. It was revived by William Farmer in 1964 and is still maintained by some scholars today, who usually call it the Two Gospel Hypothesis.

Harmony   A book that harmonizes the Gospel accounts into one. Harmonies of the Gospels have been composed since at least the second century (Tatian's *Diatessaron*) but since the eighteenth century its chief rival has been the Synopsis (q.v.).

L (Special Luke)   Material that is found in Luke alone. Sometimes 'L' (or German, *Sondergut*) is the name of the hypothetical source(s) for this material.

Luke–Acts   A term used in contemporary scholarship to refer to Luke's Gospel and the Acts of the Apostles as a two-volume work by the same author.

M (Special Matthew)   Material that is found in Matthew alone. Sometimes 'M' (or German *Sondergut*) is the name of the hypothetical source(s) for this material.

Markan posteriority	The theory that Mark knew and used Matthew and Luke (the Griesbach Theory, q.v.).
Markan Priority	The theory that Mark was the first Gospel and that this was used by both Matthew and Luke. Markan Priority is the key component of both the Two-Source Theory (q.v.) and the Farrer Theory (q.v.).
Matthaean Priority	The theory that Matthew's was the first Gospel and that it was used by Mark and Luke. It is a key element in the Griesbach Theory (q.v.).
Middle term	Used to describe the Gospel (usually Mark) that at given points stands in a mediating position among the Synoptics, that is, which agrees in major ways with the wording and order of both the other two Synoptics.
Narrative-criticism	The study of the way in which narratives are constructed, paying attention to matters of sequence, character and plot.
Patristic evidence	The evidence from the Patristic Period (second–fifth century CE)
Pericope (pl. pericopae)	A 'unit' of text, for example, Mt. 8.1-4 (the Cleansing of the Leper). The term was first used in 'form-criticism' to delineate the units that were passed on in the oral tradition.
Q	A hypothetical written source that, according to the Two-Source Theory (q.v.), was used independently by both Matthew and Luke alongside the Gospel of Mark. Q is also used as a synonym for the term 'Double Tradition' (q.v.).
Redaction-criticism	The study of the way in which authors 'redact' (edit) their source material with a view to ascertaining the literary, theological and historical viewpoint of the text and its author.
Synoptic Gospels	Matthew, Mark and Luke, but not John. They are called 'Synoptic' because they can be viewed (*opt*) together (*syn*), and thus can be arranged straightforwardly in a 'Synopsis' (q.v.).
Synoptic Problem	The study of the similarities and differences of the Synoptic Gospels in an attempt to explain their literary relationship.
Synopsis	A book that arranges Matthew, Mark and Luke in parallel columns so that the reader can analyse the degree of agreement and disagreement between them. Hence the term 'Synoptic Gospels' (q.v.).
Textual criticism	The study of the manuscripts and the textual tradition of the New Testament.
Triple Tradition	Material that is found in Matthew, Mark and Luke.

Two-Gospel Hypothesis An alternative name for the Griesbach Theory (q.v.), coined by its contemporary defenders. The idea is that Matthew and Luke are the 'Two Gospels' that were the source of Mark.

Two-Source Theory The dominant solution to the synoptic problem, whereby Matthew and Luke are held to have independently used two sources, Mark and thes hypothetical 'Q' (q.v.).

BIBLIOGRAPHY

Aland, K., *Synopsis Quattuor Evangeliorum* (Stuttgart: Deutsche Bibelgesellschaft, 15th edn, 1996, 1997).

Aland, K. (ed.), *Synopsis of the Four Gospels* (ET; Stuttgart: Deutsche Bibelgesellschaft, 1985).

Dungan, D.L., *A History of the Synoptic Problem: The Canon, the Text, the Composition and the Interpretation of the Gospels* (New York: Doubleday, 1999).

Farmer, W.R., *The Synoptic Problem: A Critical Analysis* (Macon, GA: Mercer University Press, 2nd edn, 1976).

Farrer, A., 'On Dispensing with Q', in D.E. Nineham (ed.), *Studies in the Gospel: Essays in Memory of R.H. Lightfoot* (Oxford: Basil Blackwell, 1955), pp. 55-88.

Fitzmyer, J.A., *The Gospel According to Luke: Introduction, Translation and Notes. I–IX* (Anchor Bible, 28A; New York: Doubleday, 1981).

Goodacre, M., *Goulder and the Gospels: An Examination of a New Paradigm* (JSNTSup, 133; Sheffield: Sheffield Academic Press, 1996).

—'Fatigue in the Synoptics', *NTS*44 (1998), pp. 45-58.

—*The Case Against Q: Studies in Markan Priority and the Synoptic Problem* (Harrisburg, PA: Trinity Press International, 2001).

Goulder, M.D., *Luke: A New Paradigm* (JSNTSup, 20; Sheffield: Sheffield Academic Press, 1989).

—*Midrash and Lection in Matthew* (London: SPCK, 1974).

—'Self Contradiction in the IQP', *JBL* 118 (1999), pp. 506-17.

Griesbach, J.J., *Synopsis Evangeliorum Matthaei, Marci et Lucae* (Halle, 1776).

—*Commentatio qua Marci Evangelium totum e Matthaei et Lucae commentariis decerptum esse monstratur* (A demonstration that Mark was written after Matthew and Luke) (Jena, 1789–90), in Bernard Orchard and Thomas R.W. Longstaff (eds.), *J.J. Griesbach: Synoptic and Text-Critical Studies, 1776–1976* (Cambridge: Cambridge University Press, 1978), pp. 103-35.

Head, P., *Christology and the Synoptic Problem: An Argument for Markan Priority* (SNTSMS, 94; Cambridge: Cambridge University Press, 1997).

Hengel, M., *Studies in the Gospel of Mark* (ET; London: SCM Press, 1985).

Huck, A., *Synopsis of the First Three Gospels* (rev. H. Greeven; Tübingen: J.C.B. Mohr [Paul Siebeck], 13th edn, 1981).

Johnson, Luke, *The Writings of the New Testament* (Minneapolis: Augsburg–Fortress; London: SCM Press, rev. edn, 1999 [1986]).

Kloppenborg Verbin, J., *Excavating Q: The History and Setting of the Sayings Gospel* (Minneapolis: Augsburg–Fortress; Edinburgh: T. & T. Clark, 2000).

Koester, Helmut, *Ancient Christian Gospels: Their History and Development* (London: SCM Press; Valley Forge, PA: Trinity Press International, 1990).

Kümmel, W.G., *Introduction to the New Testament* (ET; London: SCM Press, 1966).

Marxsen, W., *Introduction to the New Testament: An Approach to its Problems* (ET; Oxford: Basil Blackwell, 1968).

Neirynck, F., 'Goulder and the Minor Agreements', *ETL* 73 (1997), pp. 84-93.

Neville, D.J., *Arguments from Order in Synoptic Source Criticism: A History and Critique* (New Gospel Studies, 7; Macon, GA: Mercer University Press, 1994).

Owen, H., *Observations on the Four Gospels* (London: T. Payne, 1764).

Parker, D., *The Living Text of the Gospels* (Cambridge: Cambridge University Press, 1997).

Robinson, J.M., P. Hoffmann and J.S. Kloppenborg (eds), *The Critical Edition of Q: Synopsis Including the Gospels of Matthew and Luke, Mark and Thomas, with English, German and French Translations of Q and Thomas* (Philadelphia: Fortress Press; Leuven: Peeters, 2000).

Sanders, E.P., and M. Davies, *Studying the Synoptic Gospels* (London: SCM Press; Valley Forge, PA: Trinity Press International, 1989).

Stanton, G.N., 'Matthew, Gospel of', *DBI*, pp. 432-35.

Stein, Robert, *The Synoptic Problem: An Introduction* (Grand Rapids: Baker Book House, 1987).

Streeter, B.H., *The Four Gospels: A Study in Origins* (London: Macmillan, 1924).

Throckmorton, Burton H. Jr, *Gospel Parallels: A Comparison of the Synoptic Gospel* (Nashville, TN: Thomas Nelson, 1993).

Tuckett, C.M., *Q and the History of Early Christianity: Studies on Q* (Edinburgh: T. & T. Clark, 1996).

—'Synoptic Problem', *ABD*, VI, pp. 263-70.

Tuckett, C.M. (ed.), *The Messianic Secret* (London: SPCK; Philadelphia: Fortress Press, 1983).

INDEX OF AUTHORS

INDEX OF WORDS

THE BIBLICAL SEMINAR